READING
WITH A
SMILE
90 READING GAMES THAT WORK

The Acropolis Contemporary Education Series

READING
WITH A
SMILE
90 READING GAMES THAT WORK

Audrey Ann Burie / Mary Ann Heltshe

Foreword by JAMES E. MAUREY
Dean of Education, Millersville State College

Photos by RON BOWMAN
College Photographer, Millersville State College, Pennsylvania

PUBLISHED BY **ACROPOLIS BOOKS LTD.** • WASHINGTON, D.C. 20009

ACKNOWLEDGMENTS

Grateful acknowledgment is given to:

Educators at Millersville State College such as Dr. William Duncan, President; Dr. James Maurey, Dean of Education; Dr. Gerald Bosch, Chairman of Elementary Education; Dr. Robert Labriola, Director of the Educational Development Center; Dr. John Pflum, Director of the Elizabeth Jenkins School for Children; Dr. J. Richard Zerby, Director of Reading; and Helen Metzler, Department of Elementary Education, because of their ability to envision a meaningful education for all children and their wisdom which allows teachers to pursue quality education with confidence and freedom.

Many teachers who have encouraged us to record our ideas.

Ron Bowman, Photographer, Millersville State College, for all photographs in this book.

Mrs. Catherine Abel for her unselfish giving of time and help in preparing our manuscript.

Reprinted March, 1979

Printed in the United States of America by
Colortone Press Creative Graphics, Inc.
Washington, D.C. 20009

Library of Congress Cataloging in Publication Data

Burie, Audrey Ann, 1937-
   Reading with a smile.

   (Acropolis books for contemporary education)
   Includes indexes.
   1. Reading games.   I. Heltshe, Mary Ann, 1943-
joint author. II. Title.
LB1050.4B87   372.4'14   75-2216
ISBN 0-87491-052-8
ISBN 0-87491-053-6 pbk.   **CIP**

DEDICATION

This book is lovingly dedicated to:

The wonderful children who have shared happy classroom days and made every effort worthwhile.

Millersville State College where quality education is pursued and valued.

Our parents: Florence, John, Franny, Bill who instilled the love of learning.

Leo and Ed who give constant support and appreciation.

Little Megan whose beautiful presence gave us the opportunity to compile our ideas.

Foreword

THE PUBLICATION OF this book is not proposed as a different approach to the teaching of reading. It marks another in the progression of classroom tools that make the findings of successful classroom teachers available to other classroom teachers and interested persons. It is expected that the ideas and insight of the authors will prove to be a significant contribution to those who view reading as the basis of learning, essential for productive living, and a source of pleasure and consolation for a lifetime.

This book is designed for children from pre-school through eight years of age. The authors have achieved unity through their common focus upon individual activity which enhances basic approaches to the teaching of reading. They demonstrate and illustrate ideas which have flexibility and adaptability for use in a variety of classroom situations, and create a rich and varied climate for the development of reading skills. The illustrations are equally designed to permeate content and develop and reinforce skills in other areas; i.e., creative writing, literature, mathematics, science, and social studies.

The authors of this book, Audrey A. Burie and Mary Ann Heltshe, are to be commended for their efforts in assembling and preparing this collection for publication. Through their endeavors, the accomplishments of themselves and a number of their colleagues have been brought together for use by a broad constituency. The ideas and examples incorporated in this book are designed to make children the beneficiaries. To this end this publication is indeed a special accomplishment.

James E. Maurey, *Dean of Education*
Millersville State College

Contents

A Letter of Introduction/8

PART I   OPENING YOUR CLASSROOM WITH GAMES/9
    1 The Purposes of Reading Games/10
    2 Helpful Hints/12
    3 Supplies for Game Making/15
    4 Coding, Organizing, and Storing Games/16

PART II   READINESS GAMES/18
    5 Visual Motor/18
    6 Discrimination and Perception/22
    7 Mental Development/31

PART III   BASIC READING SKILLS GAMES/35
    8 Word Perception/36
    9 Context Clues/55
    10 Configuration/57
    11 Phonetic Analysis/58
    12 Structural Analysis/81
    13 Dictionary Skills/99
    14 Comprehension/104

PART IV   CONTENT-ORIENTED READING GAMES/109
    15 Creative Writing/110
    16 Literature/116
    17 Mathematics/119
    18 Science/129
    19 Social Studies/135
    20 Spelling/137
    Secrets for Success/139
    APPENDIX A: Patterns for Games/141
    APPENDIX B: Contract Forms and Samples/184
    Skill Index to Games/196
    General Index/200

A Letter of Introduction

Dear Teacher,

The realization of a need to put trust in our children's ability to make decisions, communicate, create and think for themselves has been long overdue in our educational system. An active child-centered classroom can be stimulating, challenging, meaningful and fun not only for children but teachers as well. The teacher who is interested in developing an open-style, child-centered program must meet three basic requirements: a commitment to provide quality education, the willingness to spend the necessary time and energy to fulfill the commitment, and the ability to listen to children in order to know their ideas and interests.

Although there are many ways and means to a child-centered classroom, we have chosen to concentrate on one area of such a program. Over a three-year period we have accumulated over two hundred reading games for instruction. These games are based upon our skill sequence in reading and cover every major area of reading concepts and skills. The enthusiastic response of children has spurred us on to create as many new activities as time and imagination permit.

We would like to share ninety of these child-tested reading games with you as well as our approach to their use in self-contained or open space classrooms. We hope that you will derive not only a wealth of materials but, more importantly, a wealth of beautiful experiences with children who are turned on to learning.

Audrey Ann Burie

Audrey Ann Burie

Mary Ann Heltshe

Mary Ann Heltshe

Part I
OPENING YOUR CLASSROOM WITH GAMES

1

The Purposes of Reading Games

A MORE FLEXIBLE CLASSROOM SETTING, whether self-contained or open space, requires that teachers initiate a definite plan to provide a balanced program. Because of its nature, the skill of reading is a vital part of almost every classroom activity and its development essential for the success of a learner. Games can provide individualized activity to that process called reading.

The value of games as an integral part of a reading program is great. In planning and making games, it is important to remember the need for flexibility and adaptability since games can be used in a variety of learning situations. Both teachers and learners reap the benefits of a rich and varied reading climate by using games.

Games are flexible in that the teacher can use a game to introduce a skill or reinforce a skill that has been part of a child's instruction. In addition to this, a game can be used to diagnose particular skill needs of a child. When a teacher uses a game as a diagnostic tool, instruction is easily individualized because only needed skills are focused upon for that child.

Games are readily adaptable for both individual and group use. They can be assigned to an individual child as part of a weekly contract (see Appendix B). The method of assigning games to individuals through a contract system fosters independence and, at the same time, "tailor-fits" instructional needs of that child.

To aid our contracting system, we use a sequence of reading skills ranging from readiness to an independent reading level. This skill sequence covers every level of competency taught in an elementary reading program. As children move through this sequence of skills, we provide games correlated with each skill area. In turn, these games are included in contract assignments thus providing consistency in areas of instruction, independent assignments, and follow-up skill work. As children progress in their independent work skills, we allow for decision making by providing them with options in selecting games. The children who are ready for this game selection keep a record on their contracts of all games completed for a given week. Since all games are coded for easy selection and storage, children find the transition from teacher-assigned games to self-selection an easy one.

At times several children may need reinforcement in a particular skill. To satisfy this need, the teacher can assign a group game to those children via their contracts.

An unexpected dividend of game usage evolved in our classroom: peer teaching! As children became familiar with games and started to work independently, they began to teach one another. After a while, children with skill strengths were seeking out and helping those children who needed help in certain skills. We then began peer teaching assignments as part of our weekly contracts.

We also found that basic reading skills were being learned through the use of content-oriented games. Many of our units in social studies and science served as a pivotal point in developing new games as children's interests were expressed.

In preparing this book for your use, we have divided the games into three major categories: readiness games, basic reading skills games, and content-oriented games. In each category we have placed a game under the specific skill for which it was made; however, you will find that most games could be used to review or extend more than one skill. With this in mind you will want to examine the "Variation" section for each game and the Skill Index to Games to determine which games will be of help to you when working with various skills in your own classroom situation.

2
Helpful Hints

PREPARING GAMES TAKES TIME and organization on the part of the teacher. In order to help you conserve time and energy, we have compiled a list of "Helpful Hints" to aid you in reaching your goals toward an activity-centered reading program. Give these hints some thought before you begin making games. Remember: "An hour saved is an additional game or two earned!"

1. Base your games on a general format or pattern with easy-to-follow directions. This will eliminate extra time spent on lengthy explanations to children. A general pattern will make game usage easier for the child.

2. Plastic freezer boxes (the type that interlock on top of one another) are ideal for individual game storage. Clear plastic shoe boxes are also great because the contents are visible at a glance. The shoe boxes are especially suitable for games with many components. These types of containers can be coded on the sides for easy reference.

3. If plastic boxes are not available to you, consider these possibilities: hosiery boxes, used pencil boxes (one gross size; ask the school secretary for these), cigar boxes, gift boxes, sandwich and individual pie serving boxes, eraser boxes.

4. If the boxes you collect are somewhat unattractive, simply cover the lids with brightly colored paper. An attractive package is far more enticing to a child than a box labeled with an advertisement for last year's erasers.

5. Be sure to label all boxes with the title of the game, and print the directions for each game as they are worded in our game format under "Directions to the Child."

6. Directions for each game should always be included even if the game is meant for a pre-reader. This explains the purpose of the game to parents, teacher aides, or other adults who may be working with a child. It is also helpful with peer teaching assignments.

7. Use clear, self-adhesive plastic to cover all game parts that are flat and mounted on posterboard, cardboard, etc. This protects your games during usage and makes your hard efforts last! You will find this plastic under such trade names as Con-tac and Kwik-Kover.

8. Mount pictures on one large sheet of posterboard when you are making a game, then cover the large piece with your clear, self-adhesive plastic. Once this is done, you can cut up the pictures into appropriate parts for your game. This is a super time-saver and it eliminates working with small pieces of adhesive plastic which can be a frustrating task! The process of protecting your work is done in one step.

9. If you are fortunate enough to have a laminating machine in your school district, be sure to make use of it. We have recently acquired one from the General Binding Sales Corporation. It has been a valuable asset to our game making, and requires less work than applying the clear, self-adhesive plastic.

10. Coding individual pieces of games on the backs or bottoms with numbers, colors, or symbols serves as a useful self-checking device for children. For example: a word card and its matching picture card could be coded on the back with the same number, color, or symbol. Colors or symbols (such as circles or triangles) work better for the younger children, but if you have a color-blind child in your class, symbols or numbers are preferable. This is not to be confused with the coding, organizing, and storing of complete games which we talk about in Chapter 4.

11. Adhesive magnetic tape—This nifty little discovery is a great way to make "characters" or animal figures come to life. (See Appendix A.) They easily adhere to a metal cabinet or magnetic board. It is a delightful way to introduce reading concepts and vocabulary to children, it saves a teacher time in writing on the chalkboard, and the game parts are usable as long as the magnet attracts! Magnetic tape can be purchased at a hobby shop and usually comes in a roll. Some educational supply houses carry this product. It cuts easily with a scissors too!

12. Be sure to assemble all of your work materials and tools before you begin. This saves time and energy when you are preparing a game.

13. Make more than one game at a time when you gather all of your tools and materials. You may wish to make one game idea in duplicate or even triplicate, especially if it will be a popular game with the children or if the skill content of the game is one you will be using often and with many children. It is also wise to wait until you have more than one game idea before you assemble all of your materials. Often you are in more of a "game making" mood than at other times. Capitalize on any surges of energy you may kindle!

14. There are many sources for pictures (besides Aunt Tillie's attic) which are useful in making the games we have suggested. Some are: old workbooks (beg the janitor not to burn them at the end of the year. Before he does, tell him it's wasteful to allow all of those treasures to go up in smoke!); magazines; coloring books (before or after you color them); children's storybooks; old basal readers; old science and social studies textbooks; beginning concept workbooks and pre-school workbooks found in drugstores and 5 & 10¢ stores; Ranger Rick magazines and the periodical issued by the National Wildlife Federation (especially good for science games); and your own Picasso-like talents.

Knowing a child's interests determines a learning program.

3

Supplies for Game Making

AN ADEQUATE SUPPLY OF MATERIALS should be kept on hand so that a lack of materials won't hinder the preparation of a game at the time of need. You will need:

1. Sources of pictures
2. Posterboard, tagboard, cardboard
3. Index cards—all sizes
4. Manila folders
5. Self-adhesive paper, clear and colored
6. Boxes
7. Colored marking pens—thin-lined and broad-pointed
8. Crayons
9. Self-adhesive labels
10. Magnetic adhesive tape
11. Self-adhesive stickers depicting cartoon and/or storybook characters to be used to make game labels more attractive.
12. Construction paper—all colors
13. A box containing tools such as scissors, rulers, glue, rubber cement, etc.
14. Manufacturers' samples such as formica tiles, fabric swatches, linoleum remnants
15. Three- and two-ply cardboard and plywood
16. Hammer, various sizes of nails, screws, hook eyes, and cup hooks. (Please store bandaids and first-aid cream for sore fingers after use of these materials.)

Please Note: Rainy days and snowy afternoons are not ideal times to go on material-gathering shopping sprees!

4

Coding, Organizing, and Storing Games

TO BE AN EFFECTIVE and efficient classroom tool, a reading skill game should be placed in a relaxed and orderly classroom setting. The implementation of reading games into a child-centered program depends upon how well children are able to use them. The basic purpose of a game and the time spent in its preparation will be lost if a child cannot function easily with it.

A child-centered classroom in which children practice both freedom and responsibility demands a subtle but firm structure provided by the teacher. Order must exist if a happy, meaningful atmosphere is to be achieved. If a child is expected to be responsible for selecting an activity, then he or she must understand the selections available and know where materials can be found and returned.

There are two basic strategies for the organization of games to provide optimum use in the classroom setting. These are a coding system and a storage system.

Young children respond to color, and a color coding system for games can be formulated. Each game is marked with a rectangular piece of colored tape or construction paper and given a number. It should be noted that the configuration of the number and the color code are the important clues to the child. A color-blind child would respond only to the numbers, so the use of both numbers and colors is important. The number is important to the teacher because each game is assigned a number on the master sheet of games available in the classroom. This master sheet containing the color codes, numbers, and names of the games becomes an easy reference when prescribing work for individualized instruction.

We used the following color scheme:

Red   -   Rhyming, Phonetic Analysis, and Structural
           Analysis Games

Blue - Classification Games
Yellow - Perception Games
Green - Math Games
Orange - Science Games
Purple - Social Studies Games.

The coding is quite helpful when preparing a child's contract. By recording the color and number of a game, the beginning reader has a guide that is easy to follow, and frustration does not occur because of unknown words in game titles.

Once a child indicates that he or she is responsible in working with a contract, more choices are introduced. Then the teacher can record the color codes of games to be played and the child can fill in the number of the game he has chosen. (See Appendix B.)

After the games have been placed in attractive containers and coded, they must be stored in a convenient location within easy reach of children. Individual wooden cubicles or cardboard boxes can be painted to correspond to the color code system. Games are then arranged so that numbers can be seen.

If closet space or an existing set of shelving is available, sections can be marked by strips of colored tape compatible with the color code. Games are then stored under the proper color.

Children need consistent encouragement and guidance when the system is introduced. Games must be returned to their proper storage area so that others can use them. Also, all game parts must be kept together. Vigilance in these areas at the start will lead to success. When a routine is established, good work habits are formed.

In our particular experience we found few game parts missing. When this did occur, everyone helped in the search immediately. However, the most rewarding outcomes were the joy in finding that individual children were making and coding games for our classroom collection and explaining to visitors just how our system operates.

Now it is time for you to select your games for production. May your efforts in establishing a more flexible program lead to many smiles in your classroom—smiles which result from a happy classroom full of meaningful activities for children.

Part II
READINESS GAMES

5
Visual Motor

TITLE: Circle Puzzles

PURPOSE:

To develop a child's perceptual skills in visual discrimination and eye-hand motor coordination skills.

MATERIALS:

Posterboard; markers; scissors; clear, self-adhesive plastic; box and label for storage.

PREPARATION:

1. Measure posterboard into 2" x 3" cards.

2. Draw circle designs on each card in duplicate form. Cover with clear, self-adhesive plastic before cutting out cards. One design will remain whole, and the other will be cut into a puzzle form.

Example:

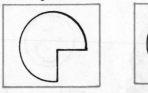 

Some example circle designs:

 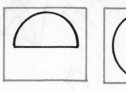 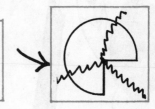

3. Store master cards and puzzle pieces in a box and label.

DIRECTIONS TO THE CHILD:

Lay all of the cards on the table. See if you can match the puzzle pieces to make the design on each card.

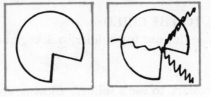

VARIATION:

Other shapes can be used in lieu of circles.

TITLE: Make a Soldier

PURPOSE:
To develop perceptual skills with the recognition and place-
ment of body parts.

MATERIALS:
Picture of a toy soldier (see Appendix A) drawn by you or
cut out of a workbook or magazine; posterboard; scissors;
glue; clear, self-adhesive plastic; box and label for storage.

PREPARATION:
1. Trace and color picture of toy soldier on posterboard,
    or mount cut out picture.
2. Cover with clear, self-adhesive plastic.
3. Cut the soldier to form a group of puzzle pieces.

4. Put in a storage box and label.

DIRECTIONS TO THE CHILD:
See if you can put our toy soldier back together again!

VARIATIONS:
It is not necessary to use a soldier. Clowns, animals, and people
of various occupations could be mounted in the same fashion and
cut up. A whole series of characters could provide a step-by-step
sequence ranging in difficulty.

TITLE: How Many Triangles?

PURPOSE:
To develop perceptual skills.

MATERIALS:
Posterboard or cardboard; markers; clear, self-adhesive plastic;
scissors; box and label for storage.

PREPARATION:
1. For use as a model and checking device, trace eight equi-
    lateral triangles and color them black. A two-inch size is
    recommended.

2. Cover with clear, self-adhesive plastic and cut out.

3. Arrange the triangles on posterboard to form a variety of
    shapes which utilize an assorted number of triangles.

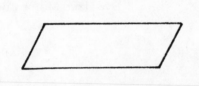

4. Trace, cover with clear plastic, and cut out the shapes.

5. As a self-checking device, mark back of each shape with
    number of triangles it uses.

6. Put shapes and black triangles in a labeled box.

DIRECTIONS TO THE CHILD:
Look at each shape. How many triangles will fit inside of
each shape you see? Lay the little black triangles ▲ on top
of the large shapes to find your answer. Look on the back
of each shape to check your answer.

VARIATION:
Use squares as the key shape and entitle the game: "How
Many Squares?"

6

Discrimination and Perception

SKILLS:
Visual Discrimination
Eye-Hand Motor Coordination

TITLE: Grid Puzzles

PURPOSE:
To develop a child's perceptual skills in visual discrimination and eye-hand motor coordination.

MATERIALS:
Manila folders; construction paper in a variety of colors; assorted colors of felt-tipped markers; white letter envelopes; glue; scissors; clear, self-adhesive plastic; ruler.

PREPARATION:
1. Mark several 1½" squares of construction paper, and cover with clear, self-adhesive plastic before cutting out.
2. Form into a grid design as shown below.

red	blue	red	blue
green	red	green	red
red	blue	red	blue
green	red	green	red
red	blue	red	blue

3.   With marking pens transfer this pattern on one side of a manila folder.

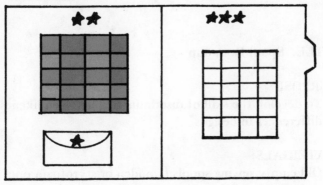

4.   Draw an empty grid with the needed amount of squares on the opposite side of the folder and cover with clear, self-adhesive plastic.

5.   Place construction paper squares in a letter envelope which you glue under the design. (This will help to keep the game pieces together). Mark game with stars as shown.

DIRECTIONS TO THE CHILD:
In the envelope with the star (*) you will find some colored squares. See if you can use those colored squares to make the design you see under the **. Put the squares in the boxes under the ***. Don't forget to put away your squares when you are finished!

VARIATIONS:
Duplicate pictures can be used and made into a puzzle form instead of squares. Once again, your own imagination is your only limitation. You can devise a number of designs to be copied by the child.

TITLE: Spool Roundup

PURPOSE:
To develop the skill of discriminating between likenesses and differences in designs.

MATERIALS:
Old empty sewing spools (wooden or styrofoam ones will do), various colored felt-tipped markers, plastic shoe box and label for storage.

PREPARATION:
1. Color in designs on a number of spools as shown below.

Examples:

2. Make a duplicate spool design for each one you've prepared. This will provide matching spool pairs.
3. Number or code matching spool bottoms for self-checking.
4. Put spools in a labeled plastic box for storage.

DIRECTIONS TO THE CHILD:
Stand up all of the spools on a table. Look at the designs on each spool. Find the spools that have the same design and match them up! Look at the bottoms of the spools to see if you are right. Count how many pairs you've matched.

VARIATIONS:
Designs may be made in triplicate so you can put four spools in a row and have the child find the design that is different.

TITLE: Match the Screws

PURPOSE:
To develop visual discrimination skills and classifying skills.

MATERIALS:
White posterboard or cardboard; fine-tipped marking pens in various colors; scissors; clear, self-adhesive plastic; box and label for storage.

PREPARATION:
1.   Line a piece of white posterboard into 2" x 2" squares.

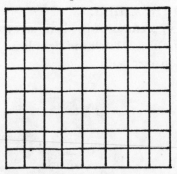

2.   Inside each square draw a picture of a screw. Vary the heads and bottoms. Variety can be obtained by coloring the heads and bottoms in different colors with markers.

Example:

3.   After you've finished drawing the screws, cover the posterboard containing your 2" x 2" pictures with clear, self-adhesive plastic.

4.   Make a master card containing a grid with the tops of the screws at the head of the vertical columns and the bottom portion of the screws at the head of the horizontal columns. Cover with plastic.

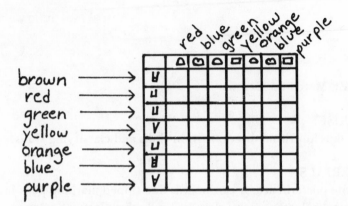

5. Cut up the 2" x 2" picture cards of the screws. These are the game pieces to be classified by the child.

6. Prepare a box and label for storage.

DIRECTIONS TO THE CHILD:

Look at the small pictures of the little screws. Find the square where the picture fits. Match the right head and bottom with its place on the master card.

TITLE: Shape Up!

PURPOSE:
To develop visual discrimination skills through perception of alike shapes.

MATERIALS:
Posterboard or construction paper; scissors; clear, self-adhesive plastic; box and label for storage.

PREPARATION:
1. Draw random shapes in duplicate form. You may wish to include simple geometric shapes in addition to the random shapes (circles, triangles, rectangles, hexagons, octagons, etc.).

2. Cover your posterboard or construction paper with clear, self-adhesive plastic before you cut out the shapes.

3. On the back, code each set of shapes for self-checking.

4. Put your shapes in a box and label.

DIRECTIONS TO THE CHILD:
Match the shapes that are exactly alike. Each shape has a match that will make a pair. Be careful—some of the shapes are tricky! Look at the numbers on the backs of the shapes to see if you are right.

VARIATION:
By cutting out pairs of shapes that are closely similar, you are providing the child with more of a challenge. Matching simple geometric shapes is an easy task. When you add irregular shapes, you are giving the child an opportunity to sharpen his perceptual skills.

TITLE: Find the Right Box

PURPOSE:
To develop the perceptual skill of estimating size.

MATERIALS:
Pictures of items that could fit into a box (old workbooks are
a good source); index cards (3" x 5"); scissors; glue; felt-tipped
markers; clear, self-adhesive plastic; box and label for storage.

PREPARATION:
1. Cut out pictures of items that could fit into a box such
   as: a hat, a baseball glove, a ball, a tie, etc. Choose items
   that vary in size, length, height, and dimension.

2. Glue these pictures on 3" x 5" index cards and cover
   with clear, self-adhesive plastic.

3. Draw pictures of boxes which would accommodate each
   item. Cover with plastic.

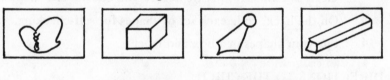

4. Code the matching item and box on the back of the
   cards as a self-checking device.

5. Put in a storage box and label.

DIRECTIONS TO THE CHILD:
Find a box for each of the items shown on the cards. Remember, the box must not be too big or too small for the item you
see on the card. Check your answers on the back of each
card when you are done. Be careful not to try fitting a hat in
a tie box!

TITLE: Alphabet Puzzle Match

PURPOSE:
To develop the skill of alphabet recognition and the matching of upper and lower case alphabet forms.

MATERIALS:
Linoleum samples (the pliable type that can be cut with a scissors); scissors; black marking pen; plastic shoe box and label for storage.

PREPARATION:
1. Cut linoleum into 26 pieces, each 2½" x 5".

2. Write each letter of the alphabet in upper case form on the left of each piece and the lower case form on the right hand side of the piece.

3. After this is done, cut each piece in the center making it a puzzle form.

4. Put all of the 52 puzzle pieces in a labeled, plastic shoe box for easy storage.

DIRECTIONS TO THE CHILD:
Match the upper case letters with the lower case letters by putting the puzzle pieces together.

VARIATIONS:
This method can be used for many skill areas: number words, color words, contractions, homographs, just to name a few!

TITLE: Alphabet Scramble

PURPOSE:
To develop alphabet recognition skills.

MATERIALS:
*52 formica sample tiles; black felt-tipped marker; plastic shoe box and label for storage; pegboard with 26 hooks.

PREPARATION:
1. On 26 formica tiles write the upper case letters of the alphabet.
2. On the remaining tiles write the lower case letters.
3. Prepare your pegboard by arranging the 26 hooks in rows.
4. Put both sets of tiles (upper and lower case letters) in a plastic shoe box for storage and label it.

DIRECTIONS TO THE CHILD:
The alphabet has been scrambled! See if you can unscramble the letters of the alphabet. First take all of the tiles out of the box. Find the ones that have upper case letters written on them. Put those letters on the pegboard hooks in ABC order. Then find the matching lower case letters which are on the rest of the tiles. Hook the lower case letters on top of the upper case letters.

*Can be found, already punched with holes, at a building supply store.

7

Mental Development

TITLE: Colorful Pet Shop

PURPOSE:
To practice color recognition skills and following directions.

MATERIALS:
Posterboard; index cards; markers (all colors); clear, self-adhesive plastic; scissors; magnetic tape (optional); envelope and label for storage.

PREPARATION:
1. Draw the outline of a pet shop on a 12" x 15" piece of posterboard and cover with clear, self-adhesive plastic before cutting out.

2. On index cards draw different kinds of pets (fish, bird, dog, etc.), color each one with magic marker, cover with plastic, and cut out. Make several animals for each of the basic colors.

3. If you have magnetic tape, it is useful to magnetize each animal and the pet shop window.

4. Print a direction card for each animal, such as: Find a purple bird.

5. Prepare a large envelope and label for storage. Also, pets and cards can be coded.

DIRECTIONS TO THE CHILD:
1. (If an adult and child are playing the game) Put the animals in the pet shop window. Then, listen, and I will ask you to take certain pets out of the pet shop.

2. (For independent use) Put the animals in the pet shop window. Then read each direction card and find the pet to match it. Read the cards to someone when you have finished.

TITLE: Dilemma Dillies

PURPOSE:
To develop the thinking skill of problem solving on the readiness level.

MATERIALS:
Posterboard or 5" x 8" index cards; felt-tipped markers; clear, self-adhesive plastic; scissors; 3" x 5" index cards; box and label for storage.

PREPARATION:
1. On a 5" x 8" index card draw, in simple form, figures to depict a problem situation.

2. On a 3" x 5" index card draw a picture of an item that will solve the problem. Then provide three optional pictures of items that would not be suitable to solve the problem. Pictures from old workbooks could be used in lieu of drawings.

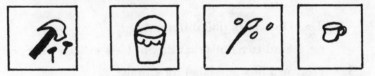

3. Draw as many dilemmas as you can think of on 5" x 8" cards. Provide possible solutions on 3" x 5" cards to go with each dilemma.

4. Cover all pictures with clear, self-adhesive plastic. Code backs of matching cards for self-checking. Put them in a storage box and label your game.

DIRECTIONS TO THE CHILD:
We have some dilemma dillies! On each of the large cards you will see pictures of people with a problem. You can help them solve their dilemmas by finding just the right item to help solve their problem. Turn cards over to check yourself. Be careful or you may become a dilemma dillie!

TITLE: Rag Doll Dress-Up

PURPOSE:
To give children practice with perceptual and discrimination skills and following directions.

MATERIALS:
Posterboard or felt in a variety of colors; rag doll patterns (see Appendix A); markers; scissors; index cards; clear, self-adhesive plastic (optional); box and label for storage.

PREPARATION:
1. Make a double set of rag dolls and clothes from poster-board or felt. If posterboard is used, cover with clear, self-adhesive plastic before cutting out.

2. Prepare direction cards by writing a direction on each index card.

    Examples are:
    a. Find two dolls that look alike.
    b. Dress the two dolls exactly alike.
    c. Dress one doll in something you might wear to swim.
    d. Dress each doll differently.
    e. Find two dolls that do not look exactly alike, etc.

3. Prepare a box and label for storage.

DIRECTIONS TO THE CHILD:
We are going to play a dress-up game. Let's see if you can do certain things with these dolls and the clothes. (The adult then reads each direction to the child.)

VARIATIONS:
Seasonal and/or weather types of clothing could be added. Color discrimination could be included in the direction cards also. Children who have begun to read could handle direction cards by themselves.

Part III
BASIC READING SKILLS GAMES

8

Word
Perception

TITLE: Matching at the Zoo

PURPOSE:
To study meanings of words and match them with concrete objects.

MATERIALS:
Plastic zoo animal models; posterboard; scissors; markers; box and label for storage.

PREPARATION:
1. Cut 2" x 2" strips from posterboard.
2. Print the name for each animal on a strip.
3. Code the back of each strip and the matching animal with a corresponding number or design.
4. Store animals and strips in a labeled box.

DIRECTIONS TO THE CHILD:
Take the plastic zoo animals and set them up on a table. Find the card which has the animal's name on it and match it with each animal. Check yourself. Remember: Please don't feed the animals!

VARIATIONS:
A set of farm animals, pre-historic animals, etc., could be used in the same fashion. Another variation is to use consonant letters instead of words and you have a manipulative beginning sounds of letters game.

TITLE: A Breakfast Puzzle

PURPOSE:
To practice visual perception skills by using common words for everyday household articles.

MATERIALS:
Cereal boxes (small individual boxes are good to use); scissors; box and label for storage.

PREPARATION:
1. Cut each box front into puzzle pieces.
2. Make straight edges rather than jigsaw-type pieces.

3. Prepare a box and label for storage.

DIRECTIONS TO THE CHILD:
Have a breakfast treat! See how many cereal boxes you can put together. Then read the name of each kind of cereal.

VARIATIONS:
The same idea could be used with any box from a household article. However, be sure that the product is a familiar one to a child.

TITLE: Food Group Match

PURPOSE:
To develop classification skills and word recognition.

MATERIALS:
Pictures of foods from the four basic food groups; posterboard; scissors; markers; glue; clear, self-adhesive plastic; box
and label for storage.

PREPARATION:

1. Cut out pictures of various foods which can be found in
   discarded magazines.

2. Mount pictures on posterboard. Be sure to write the
   name of the food under each picture.

3. Cover with clear, self-adhesive plastic and cut into cards.

4. On the back of each card write the correct category as a
   self-checking device.

5. Make four category cards larger in size than the picture
   cards. Cover with plastic.

6. Cut up food cards and store in a box with category cards.

DIRECTIONS TO THE CHILD:
Look at each of the pictures and think of the kind of food it
is. Put all of the meat group foods together, the fruits and
vegetables together, dairy products together, and the bread
and cereal foods together. Check your answers on the back of
each card.

TITLE: Let's Eat

PURPOSE:
To match the names of common or favorite foods with their picture.

MATERIALS:
Magazine pictures; posterboard; magic markers; scissors; glue; clear, self-adhesive plastic; box and label for storage.

PREPARATION:
1. Find pictures of foods such as: spaghetti and meatballs, mashed potatoes and gravy, macaroni and cheese, corn on the cob, chicken pie, pizza pie, hot dogs and baked beans, etc.

2. On posterboard measure 3" x 4" rectangles. Mount pictures on rectangles, cover with plastic, and cut.

3. Measure posterboard into 1" x 4" strips. Print the name or phrase for each food on a strip, cover with plastic, and cut.

4. Code the back of picture and name card for self-checking.

5. Prepare a box and label for storage.

DIRECTIONS TO THE CHILD:
Look at the pictures of foods we like. See if you can match the word card for each one. Don't try to eat them! Check yourself.

VARIATIONS:
The kinds of pictures used should be familiar to the group of children with whom you work. Another adaptation would be to group pictures and words according to particular countries or ethnic groups.

TITLE: Animal ABC

PURPOSE:
To strengthen word recognition skills and develop alphabetizing skills.

MATERIALS:
Posterboard; pictures of animals (workbooks are a good source); glue; scissors; felt-tipped markers; clear, self-adhesive plastic; box and label for storage.

PREPARATION:
1. Measure posterboard into 3" squares, and mount a picture of an animal on each square.

2. Cover posterboard with clear, self-adhesive plastic and then cut out the squares.

3. Try to find animals that have names which begin with each letter of the alphabet. Here is a sample list:

Antelope	Hippopotamus	Newt	Tiger
Bear	Ibis	Octopus	Unicorn
Cat	Jaguar	Pig	Viper
Deer	Kangaroo	Quail	Wolf
Elephant	Lion	Rabbit	Yak
Fox	Monkey	Seal	Zebra
Giraffe			

4. Measure posterboard into 2" x 4" strips. On each strip write an animal's name. Cover with plastic before cutting out strips.

5. Code pictures and names for self-checking, and put pictures and name cards in a labeled box for storage.

DIRECTIONS TO THE CHILD:
Sort out all of the animal pictures. Find a name card to go with each animal picture. Look on the backs of pictures and cards to check yourself. When you have done this, put the animal name cards in ABC order. Try putting the pictures in ABC order without looking at their names. Watch out for the wild ones!

VARIATIONS:
You can use any classification of items as the base of this game. Household items, toys, foods, articles of clothing all lend themselves well to this type of game.

TITLE: Feed Benny Bear

PURPOSE:
To reinforce word recognition skills.

MATERIALS:
Posterboard; Benny Bear and honey pot patterns (see Appendix A); markers; clear, self-adhesive plastic; index cards (4" x 6" size); scissors; adhesive magnetic tape; vocabulary list; poster or tempera paints (optional); box and label for storage.

PREPARATION:
1. Trace the form of Benny Bear on posterboard. You may wish to paint Benny with markers or paints. Then cover him with clear, self-adhesive paper before you cut him out.

2. Magnetize Benny Bear with adhesive magnetic tape.

3. On 4" x 6" index cards trace a honey pot pattern. Use this pattern to make as many pots as there are words on your list.

4. Write a word on each honey pot. Then cover each pot with clear, self-adhesive plastic before cutting out and magnetizing each pot.

5. Put Benny Bear and the honey pots in a large box and label the game.

41

DIRECTIONS TO THE CHILD:

Find a spot to hang Benny Bear. See how many pots of honey you can feed Benny Bear. Look at each word written on the honey pots. If you can read the word, put it next to Benny Bear. You may want to play this game with a friend! See who can feed Benny the most pots of honey!

VARIATIONS:

This game may be used as a teacher-directed activity, a peer-teaching device, an individual game, or a group word game.

The honey pots could contain: phrases, rhyming words, words with blends and digraphs to be reviewed, homonyms to be matched, synonyms to be matched.

Reading is a vital part of almost every classroom activity.

TITLE: Worm Word Circles

PURPOSE:
To add variety and interest in presenting and drilling word recognition skills.

MATERIALS:
Posterboard; clear, self-adhesive plastic; felt-tipped markers; scissors; magnetic tape; list of words to be introduced; pattern for worm's head (see Appendix A); box and label for storage.

PREPARATION:
1. Trace on posterboard the number of circles (using worm's head as your model) needed to accommodate the words on your list.

2. Cover the circles with clear, self-adhesive plastic after you have written your words on them. Cut out each circle and magnetize it with magnetic tape.

3. Trace worm's head, cover with plastic, cut it out, and apply magnetic tape.

4. Prepare a box and label for storage.

DIRECTIONS TO THE CHILD:
See if you can build a worm! Find a friend to play this game. Look at each circle and read the word you see. Be careful to look at the letter sounds in the word. Once you have read the word, check it with your friend. Add the body part to the worm's head. Do this until you've read all of the words.

VARIATIONS:
This game lends itself well as a teacher-directed activity, especially for initial word introduction. Here are some clever variations of the word circles: a balloon and strings, lollipops and pop sticks, ice cream scoop and cone. A magnetic chalkboard would be helpful for these variations.

TITLE: Watch the Signs!

PURPOSE:
To develop word recognition skills by using words found in the child's environment.

MATERIALS:
List of words from signs found in a child's environment; posterboard; felt-tipped markers; popsicle sticks; glue; clay; old workbooks or magazines; scissors; clear, self-adhesive plastic; box and label for storage.

PREPARATION:

1. Make three dimensional signs out of posterboard, popsicle sticks, and clay. Try to make your replicas as close to the real signs as possible.

2. Make 2" x 3" cards with the words from the signs written on them. Cover with plastic before cutting out.

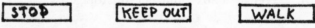

3. From the old workbooks and/or magazines, cut out pictures depicting the command indicated by the signs (i.e., *walk*—a picture of a person walking; *in*—a picture of a person entering a building or place; *watch for children*—a picture of children playing in a street or along a sidewalk). Mount them on posterboard and cover with clear, self-adhesive plastic before cutting up into cards.

4. Measure several 2" x 10" strips on posterboard. On these strips write sentences using words on the signs. Leave a blank where the word should be placed. Cover with plastic and cut out.

Example: We left the theater by going through the door marked *(exit)*.

(Stop) and look before you cross the street.

NOTE: The 2" x 3" word cards can be used for this step of the game to fill in the blanks.

5. Some common signs found in a child's environment might include these words:

exit	do not enter
stop	in
go	out
walk	step down
children playing	slow
keep off the grass	watch for children
caution	danger

6. Put three dimensional signs, 2" x 3" cards, picture cards, and sentence cards in a box for storage and label.

DIRECTIONS TO THE CHILD:

Step 1:   Take out the little signs and stand them up on the floor or on a table. Match the signs up with the word cards. See if you can find the same words on the signs.

Step 2:   Sort out the picture cards. On each card you will see people doing what the signs say. Match the pictures with the right signs and word cards.

Step 3:   Read each of the sentence strips. There is a word missing in each sentence. Think of the missing word— you will find it among the word cards. Put the word card on the blank to make the sentence complete.

VARIATION:

This game can be used to meet individual needs because of the various steps. Step one involves matching, step two is more difficult because the child must read the sign and word card, and step three is the most difficult because of the context clues and sentence reading. You can assign only one step or more with this game!

TITLE: Ring the Words

PURPOSE:
To develop the skill of recognizing synonyms.

MATERIALS:
Posterboard; felt-tipped markers; scissors; clear, self-adhesive plastic; rubber jar rings used for canning; list of synonyms; box and label for storage.

PREPARATION:
1. Cut strips out of posterboard measuring 3" x 12".
2. On these strips write four words—three synonyms and one that is not a synonym.

3. Cover each strip with clear, self-adhesive plastic and store in a box with the rubber rings.

DIRECTIONS TO THE CHILD:
Look at all of the words written on each strip. Find the one word that does not belong with the others. Three of the words have the same meaning; one does not. After you have found the one that doesn't belong, put a rubber ring around it. Do the same with all of the strips of words.

VARIATION:
This game can be used with antonyms. Just have the child put rings around the pair of opposites.

TITLE: A Mug of Synonyms

PURPOSE:
To extend the meanings of words through the use of synonyms.

MATERIALS:
White posterboard or oaktag; mug and packet patterns (see
Appendix A); markers; clear, self-adhesive plastic; scissors;
razor blade; box and label for storage.

PREPARATION:
1. Trace five mugs and fifteen packets (these are to be
    made to resemble the hot chocolate mix). Use poster-
    board or oaktag.

2. Decorate each mug and write a word across the center of
    each. Cover with plastic before cutting out. Slit the
    mouth of each cup with a razor blade so that packets
    can be placed in the openings. Words which can be used
    are:

clear

pretty   SLIT

happy   sad   dark

3. Outline each packet and place a synonym on each one.
    Cover with plastic and cut out. Make three synonym
    packets for each mug. Words are:

unhappy   gay   Transparent

glad   lovely   black   glum   etc.

4. Code mugs and packs for self-checking.
5. Prepare a box and label for storage.

DIRECTIONS TO THE CHILD:
Fill the mugs with synonyms! Match each word pack with a
word on a mug with the same meaning. Place each pack in
the slit of a mug. Check yourself!

TITLE: Catch a Baby Kangaroo

PURPOSE:
To practice identifying words with opposite meanings.

MATERIALS:
Posterboard (any color); kangaroo and baby pattern (see Appendix A); felt-tipped markers; clear, self-adhesive plastic; scissors; razor blade; box and label for storage.

PREPARATION:
1. Trace twelve mother kangaroos and twelve babies onto posterboard.
2. Fill in details with markers.
3. Print a word on each mother kangaroo and its opposite on a baby.

4. Suggested antonyms are: in-out, up-down, on-off, black-white, top-bottom, pretty-ugly, happy-sad, give-take, dark-light, rain-shine, come-go, yes-no.
5. Cover with plastic and cut out.
6. Slit each mother's pouch with a razor blade so that a baby can easily fit into it.
7. Code the back of each baby and mother with a number or design for self-checking.
8. Prepare a box and label for storage.

DIRECTIONS TO THE CHILD:
Help the mother kangaroos to find their babies. Read the word on each mother and find the baby that has a word which means the opposite. Put the baby in the mother's pouch.

VARIATIONS:
The game could be used by two children or a small instructional group. Several mothers and babies could be made with no words and children could make up their own. A grease pencil over lamination or clear adhesive will easily wipe off.

TITLE: Tasty Homonyms

PURPOSE:
To practice the use of homonyms.

MATERIALS:
Brown posterboard or construction paper; gingerbread figure pattern (see Appendix A); magnetic tape; white index cards; thin-lined marker; colored markers; scissors; clear, self-adhesive plastic; box and label for storage.

PREPARATION:
1. Trace 10 gingerbread figures on posterboard or construction paper.
2. Fill in facial details and decorate each figure, except for the center.
3. Cover with plastic and cut out.
4. Cut magnetic tape into ¼" to ½" pieces. Place 2 pieces on each gingerbread figure where icing or raisins are usually found.
5. Outline 20 button-like or icing-like pieces, about ¾" round, on index cards. Fill in with colored markers.

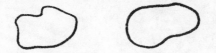

6. Print homonyms on each piece. Cover with plastic and cut out. Be sure to have 10 pairs!

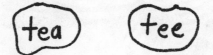

   Words which can be used are: him-hymn, tea-tee, made-maid, sea-see, pair-pear, doe-dough, deer-dear, I-eye, tow-toe, fair-fare.
7. Code the backs of the homonym pieces for self-checking. Place magnetic tape on the back of each piece.
8. Prepare a box and label for storage.

DIRECTIONS TO THE CHILD:

Be a baker! Decorate each gingerbread figure with a pair of homonyms. Check yourself. Don't eat any! They're made of paper!

VARIATIONS:

This game could be mounted and used as a learning center. It would be appropriate to use at Christmastime. You might have children compose sentences either orally or in print to show the various meanings of homonym words.

Enjoyment of reading leads to a rich and varied life style.

TITLE: Meanings Galore

PURPOSE:
To extend vocabulary through the use of words with multiple meanings.

MATERIALS:
Posterboard; old magazines or workbooks; marker; scissors; glue; clear, self-adhesive plastic; 3-D objects (explained below); box and label for storage.

PREPARATION:
1. Cut at least five 6" x 9" posterboard pieces.
2. On the bottom of each one write a word which has more than one meaning such as band, fly, bat, ball, and check.
3. Find and mount pictures on posterboard rectangles which illustrate the meanings of these words or find a 3-D object such as a rubber band or rubber ball.
4. Master cards and picture cards may be covered with plastic.
5. Code objects, picture cards, and master cards for self-checking.
6. Prepare a box and label for storage.

DIRECTIONS TO THE CHILD:
Place the five cards in front of you. Take the objects and pictures and put them on the card which has a word to describe it. Check yourself. Notice how many different meanings a word can have.

VARIATION:
Sentences on strips can be added to each picture or object.

TITLE: Find My Grandchildren

PURPOSE:
To help children recognize and classify idioms of speech.

MATERIALS:
Posterboard; Grandfather and Grandchild Bunny pattern (see Appendix A); index cards; felt-tipped markers; scissors; clear, self-adhesive plastic; list of idioms; box and label for storage.

PREPARATION:
1. Make a pattern of "Grandfather Bunny" and his "grand-child." Trace these on posterboard making as many bunnies as needed for all the idioms on your list. Each "Grandfather" will contain the first part of the idiom. The "grandchildren" will contain the nouns that fit into the descriptive category of the idiom.

2. Cover the bunnies with clear, self-adhesive plastic before cutting them out.

3. Some examples of idioms are:

    > As soft as . . . silk, a pillow, cotton, fur, etc.
    > As hard as . . . a rock, a board, cement, a stone, etc.
    > As light as . . . a feather, air, an empty box, etc.
    > As big as . . . an elephant, a giant, a tall tree, etc.
    > As hungry as . . . a horse, a bear, etc.
    > As tiny as . . . an ant, a flea, etc.
    > As quiet as . . . snow, a mouse, etc.
    > As pretty as . . . a flower, a picture, etc.

4. Code backs of grandfather-grandchildren for self-checking.

5. Prepare box and label for storage.

DIRECTIONS TO THE CHILD:

Help the grandfather bunnies find their grandchildren! Read the phrase on each grandfather bunny; then find the words to complete the phrases. Look at the backs to check yourself.

TITLE: As Easy as Pie

PURPOSE:
To practice the use of figurative speech.

MATERIALS:
Posterboard (any color); scissors; marker (black); pictures from old magazines and workbooks; glue (optional); clear, self-adhesive plastic; box and label for storage.

PREPARATION:
1. Measure twelve 3" x 5" strips of posterboard.

2. On each strip print a phrase. Examples are:

    as easy as
    as light as a
    as soft as

3. Cover with plastic and cut out.

4. On twelve 3" x 3" squares of posterboard glue or draw pictures which would correspond to the phrases. Cover with plastic before cutting.

as easy as

as light as a

5. Code the phrases and matching pictures on the back.
6. Prepare box and label for storage.

DIRECTIONS TO THE CHILD:
Read each phrase on the cards. See if you can find a picture to go with each one. Check yourself by looking on the back of the card and picture.

VARIATION:
This particular activity may be used as a group game.

9

Context Clues

TITLE: Cones for Sale

PURPOSE:
To aid in developing comprehension skills through paragraph and title match.

MATERIALS:
Posterboard; ice cream cone pattern (see Appendix A); fine-line markers; clear, self-adhesive plastic; scissors; collection of paragraphs and titles appropriate to reading level needed; box and label for storage.

PREPARATION:
1. Draw the shape of an ice cream cone and use it as a pattern. Trace your pattern on posterboard giving yourself as many cones as needed for your stories or paragraphs.

2. On the base of each ice cream cone print a short story or paragraph and on the ice cream portion write the accompanying title.

3. Cover the cones with clear, self-adhesive plastic; then cut them out.

4. Cut the ice cream portion from the base of each cone.

5. Code backs of pairs for self-checking.

6. Store cones and ice cream tops in a box and label the game.

DIRECTIONS TO THE CHILD:

See how many ice cream cones you can buy! Just read the stories written on each of the cones, then find the right name of the story on the ice cream dips. Match each story with the correct title. Check yourself by looking at the backs of cones and dips. When you match the cones and the dips, you have bought them! Play this game with a friend and see who buys the most ice cream cones! Don't get sick eating too much ice cream!

VARIATIONS:

This technique can apply to any reading level or reading skill. Riddles or simple sentences can be matched with a word. Plurals, contractions, or possessives can also be used as the core of this game.

10
Configuration

TITLE: Take a Ride on Little Toot!

PURPOSE:
To develop the skill of recognizing configuration clues.

MATERIALS:
Posterboard; markers; clear, self-adhesive plastic; index cards; scissors; box and label for storage; list of words with varying configurations.

PREPARATION:
1. Draw train cars on posterboard to correlate with the configurations of the words on your list.

2. Cover cars with clear, self-adhesive plastic; then cut them out. These train cars will be the masters for sorting and discriminating configurations of the words on your list.

3. Write words that match the shapes of the train cars on index cards. Cover them with clear, self-adhesive plastic.

4. Code cars and index cards for self-checking.

5. Store cards and train parts in a box.

DIRECTIONS TO THE CHILD:
Lay Little Toot out on the floor. Take the word cards and put them in a pile. Take the top card from the pile and look at the word. Trace around the word with your finger. Can you see the shape of the word? Now find a car in Little Toot's train that has the same shape as the word on the card. When you have found it, lay the word card on top of the car in Little Toot's train. Do the same with all of the other word cards. Look at the backs of cars and cards to see if you are right. Find some friends and play the game with them! Hope you enjoy your ride on Little Toot's Express!

11

Phonetic Analysis

TITLE: Rhyming Clowns

PURPOSE:
To give child practice in rhyming words.

MATERIALS:
Posterboard; markers; clown pattern (see Appendix A); clear, self-adhesive plastic; paper fasteners; scissors; razor blade; box and label for storage.

PREPARATION:
1.   Draw two clowns on posterboard and fill in the details.

slot — Happy #1

slot — Slappy #2

2. Make two corresponding discs with rhyming pairs on each disc.

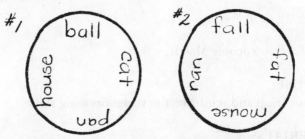

3. Cover clowns and discs with plastic before cutting out.
4. With a razor blade make a slot in the clowns' mouths so that a rotating disc will fit into each one.
5. Insert the discs in the mouths of the clowns. Fasten with a brass fastener.

6. Make reserve discs to be interchanged. They may vary in difficulty.
7. Prepare box and label for storage.

DIRECTIONS TO THE CHILD:
Happy and Slappy are twin clowns. They each know some rhyming words. See if you can make Happy and Slappy say a rhyming pair of words at the same time!

TITLE: Snowpeople Match

PURPOSE:
To develop and reinforce the visual rhyming skill.

MATERIALS:
Index cards; snowperson pattern (see Appendix A); markers; clear, self-adhesive plastic; scissors; list of rhyming words; box and label for storage.

PREPARATION:
1. Trace several snowpeople on index cards.

2. On their bodies write several sets of words to be put in a rhyming sequence.

3. Code the backs of rhyming snowpeople for self-checking.

4. Cover the snowpeople with clear, self-adhesive plastic before cutting them out. Then store them in a box and label.

DIRECTIONS TO THE CHILD:
Help the snowpeople find their friends! Put them in order by finding the words on their tummies that rhyme. Be quick and time yourself. Put the snowpeople that rhyme together, before they melt! Look on the backs of snowpeople to check yourself.

TITLE: Make a Word Family

PURPOSE:
To develop the skill of using linguistic word patterns and rhyming.

MATERIALS:
Linoleum pieces (the pliable type which can be cut with a scissors) or posterboard; markers; list of rhyming words; scissors; plastic shoe box and label.

PREPARATION:
1. Cut linoleum or posterboard into two sizes (1" x 2") and (3" x 2").

2. Write beginning sounds on the 1" x 2" pieces and word families on the 3" x 2" pieces.

3. Make duplicate letters (1" x 2" size) for frequently used initial consonants and be sure to include a variety of word families.

4. Store letter cards and endings in a plastic shoe box.

DIRECTIONS TO THE CHILD:
See how many word families you can find. Match the first sounds on the smaller cards with a word family ending on the larger cards to make words. Count how many "members" each family has. Which word family is the largest?

61

TITLE: Toyland Jamboree

PURPOSE:
To develop auditory recognition of initial consonant sounds.

MATERIALS:
Posterboard; markers; pictures of toys; glue; scissors; clear, self-adhesive plastic; box and label for storage.

PREPARATION:
1. Convert a piece of posterboard into a "toy shop."

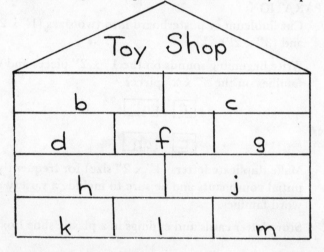

2. Line a piece of posterboard into 3" x 3" squares. Then glue a beginning sound toy picture inside each square to correspond with the letter sounds on the shelves of your "toy store."

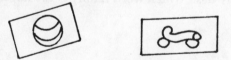

3. Cover the pictures with clear, self-adhesive plastic; then cut them up.

4. Code backs of picture cards with letters for self-checking.

5. Put the pictures in a labeled storage box.

DIRECTIONS TO THE CHILD:

Let's go shopping in a toy store! Before you can ~~buy~~ must put the toys on the right shelf. Look at each toy and say its name out loud. Listen for the first sound; then find a shelf in the toy store that has that letter sound written on it. Put all the toys on the right shelves. Look on the backs of cards to check yourself. To "buy" the toys you must give another word with the same beginning sound of the toy you want to buy.

Have fun and be sure not to mix up the dolls with the teddy bears!

TITLE: Digraph Fun

PURPOSE:
To practice using and locating digraphs in the initial and final position of words.

MATERIALS:
Old magazines or workbooks; posterboard; scissors; paste; clear, self-adhesive plastic; box and label for storage.

PREPARATION:
1. Find pictures of objects which begin or end with the digraphs—sh, th, ch, wh.

2. Paste the pictures on posterboard, which has been measured into 3" squares.

3. Print the digraphs on 2" x 3" posterboard strips. Use a line to show initial or final position.

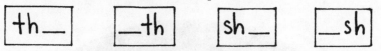

4. Cover squares and strips with plastic before cutting.

5. Code the backs for self-checking.

6. Prepare a box and label for storage.

DIRECTIONS TO THE CHILD:
How well do you know the digraph sounds? Say the name of each picture. Listen to see if the digraph sound is at the beginning or end of the word. Place the card which shows this under the picture. Turn the picture over and check yourself.

VARIATIONS:
Plastic objects could be used in place of pictures. Also, other digraph sounds such as: ____ng, ____nk, and ph could be used if the children are advanced in this phonetic skill.

TITLE: Help to Brew the Witches' Stews

PURPOSE:
To reinforce sounds associated with blends. (Examples: br, gl, st, pr, cr, cl, etc.)

MATERIALS:
Posterboard; witch and pot pattern (see Appendix A); scissors; markers; magnetic tape; clear, self-adhesive plastic; old workbooks or magazines; paste; razor blade; box and label for storage.

PREPARATION:
1. Make at least six witches. Cover with plastic before cutting.
2. Slit the cauldron top with the razor blade.
3. Make little labels of blends st_, etc., and attach to the cauldron with tape or magnetic tape. In this way, you can use the same idea with any of the blend sounds you may want to introduce or practice.
4. Find pictures which illustrate the sounds of the blends you have chosen.
5. Mount pictures on posterboard, measured into 2" x 3" rectangles. Cover with plastic before cutting.
6. Code backs of pictures with blends for self-checking.
7. Prepare a box and label for storage.

DIRECTIONS TO THE CHILD:
Help the witches brew their stews. Say the name of each picture and put it in the pot which shows the letters of the blend you hear at the beginning of the word. Check yourself. Please don't fall into any pot!

VARIATION:
Substitute warlocks for witches.

TITLE: Hukilau

PURPOSE:
To practice the use of the sounds of hard and soft c and g.

MATERIALS:
Construction paper; posterboard; markers; palm tree and fish pattern (see Appendix A); travel folders of Hawaii or old magazines; scissors; glue; clear, self-adhesive plastic; envelope and label for storage.

PREPARATION:
1. Cut a 12" x 15" piece of posterboard and, using travel folder of Hawaii or pictures from magazines, create a Hawaiian beach scene. (If you don't feel so ambitious just use a few palm trees.)

2. Along the beach line, mark off four fish nets and label hard c, soft c, hard g, soft g. Cover with plastic.

3. Make fish from construction paper and print hard and soft c and g words on each one you make. Cover with plastic before cutting.

4. Suggested word list: cent, city, circus, citizen, catch, car, camel, cat, go, gallon, get, gum, gentleman, gym, gypsy.

5. Code backs of fish with correct sound for self-checking.

6. Prepare an envelope and label for storage.

DIRECTIONS TO THE CHILD:
You are invited to a Hawaiian Hukilau. Place the fish in the sea. Look at each word. Read it. Then put each fish into the correct net. Check yourself. Have fun! Aloha!

TITLE: Early Birds

PURPOSE:
To practice the short vowel sounds in words.

MATERIALS:
Posterboard; construction paper; word list; felt-tipped markers; bird in nest and worm pattern (see Appendix A); scissors; razor blade; clear, self-adhesive plastic; box and label for storage.

PREPARATION:

1. Trace five "Bird in Nest" figures.

2. Color and fill in details with markers.

3. Print a vowel letter with the breve on each.

4. Cover with plastic before cutting.

5. Using a razor blade, make a slit in the center of the nest along the black line between the body of the bird and the nest.

6. Trace about 24 worms onto pink construction paper and outline them with a marker.

7. Print a short vowel word on each one. Cover with plastic and cut.

8. The back can be marked with the correct vowel, for self-checking.

9. Possible words are apple, battle, catch, hat, tan, Eddie, felt, head, said, set, kit, little, pig, ship, bottom, dog, happily, top, cup, honey, hunt, gun, puppy.

10. Prepare a box and label for storage.

DIRECTIONS TO THE CHILD:

Early birds try for worms. Help the mothers to feed the nestlings. Find the worms to match the vowels and put them in the correct nests. Check yourself!

VARIATION:

After the children have placed the worms, they should read the words aloud to someone. This game is effective as a learning center. Worms can be kept in a grass strip at the bottom of the center within easy reach of the children. Long vowel sounds can be used as well.

TITLE: The Long and Short of It

PURPOSE:
To practice the use of the following long and short vowel
rules:
1. Two vowels together
2. Vowel-consonant-e
3. One vowel between 2 consonants

MATERIALS:
Posterboard (any color); markers; scissors; dog pictures; paste
(optional); clear, self-adhesive plastic; white index cards; box
or large envelope and a label for storage.

PREPARATION:
1. Draw two doghouses on posterboard.

2. Label one "Long" and one "Short."

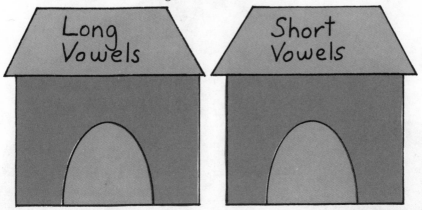

3. Paste or draw a picture of
   a dog on each doghouse.

4. Make a set of dog bones
   from the white index cards.

5. Place a word with a long or
   short vowel sound on each bone.

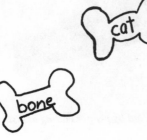

69

6. Cover doghouses and bones with plastic before cutting them. Bones may be labeled "long" and "short" on back for self-checking.

7. Prepare a box and label for storage.

DIRECTIONS TO THE CHILD:

Read the words on each bone. Place the bones under the right doghouse. Look on the backs of bones to check yourself. Don't bury any!

VARIATIONS:

This game could serve as an excellent instructional group game when vowel rules are being studied. Using strips of magnetic tape on the back of houses and bones is useful if you have a magnetic chalkboard.

Contract work is simplified by proper coding and storage.

TITLE: Catch the Raindrops

PURPOSE:
To develop the skill of recognizing long and short vowel sounds.

MATERIALS:
Posterboard; markers; umbrella and raindrop patterns (see Appendix A); plastic bucket to store "raindrops" during game play; scissors; clear, self-adhesive plastic; label and a large box, container, or envelope for storage of game; adhesive magnetic tape; two lists of words—one containing long vowel words and one with short vowel words.

PREPARATION:
1. Make two umbrella shapes out of posterboard, and mark one "Long Vowels" and one "Short Vowels." Cover shapes with clear, self-adhesive plastic before cutting.

2. Magnetize each umbrella by applying magnetic tape on the back of each umbrella.

3. Make raindrops to correspond with number of words on your word lists.

4. Write words on raindrops and cover them with clear, self-adhesive plastic before cutting.

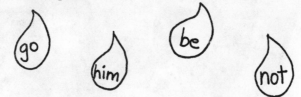

5. Code backs of raindrops with "long" or "short" for self-checking, and magnetize raindrops with adhesive magnetic tape.

71

6. Store umbrella and raindrops in a box or envelope and label the game. Keep a plastic bucket with game supplies to be used in playing this game.

DIRECTIONS TO THE CHILD:

You can play this game by yourself or with a friend. Put the raindrops in the plastic bucket. Put the long and short umbrellas on a magnetic board. Reach in the bucket and pull out a raindrop. Read the word written on the raindrop. Listen for the vowel sound in that word. Is it long or short? Match the raindrop with the right umbrella. Do the same for each raindrop until the rainstorm is over! Look on backs of raindrops to check yourself.

VARIATIONS:

Word Recognition
Vowel Dipthongs and Digraphs
Opposites

NOTE: Children become familiar with using magnetic-type games for peer teaching and they will readily seek a spot in the classroom where there is a magnetic surface such as: a file cabinet, magnetic chalkboard, or the side of a metal desk.

TITLE: Save the Bunnies

PURPOSE:
To practice four of the rules associated with the use of vowel sounds.

MATERIALS:
Posterboard (4 colors); index cards; markers; scissors; clear, self-adhesive plastic; hunter and rabbit patterns (see Appendix A); box and label for storage.

PREPARATION:
1. Trace four hunter silhouettes, using a different color for each one.
2. Print a vowel rule and sample word on each.
   (a) Two vowels together, long: feed.
   (b) Vowel-consonant-e, long: cake.
   (c) One vowel at the end, long: go.
   (d) Consonant-vowel-consonant, short: hat.

3. Trace approximately 16 rabbits onto index cards. Outline figures and fill in facial features.
4. Print a word on each body which follows one of the above rules. Suggested words are keep, bait, coat, hi, yoke, tea, me, hop, pot, like, clean, same, fun, cab, tin, so.

5. Cover hunter and bunnies with plastic before cutting out.
6. Code backs of bunnies for self-checking.
7. Prepare a box and label for storage.

DIRECTIONS TO THE CHILD:

Help "Little Running Deer" and friends save the bunnies.
Place the bunnies behind the hunter who has the correct rules
for the word on a bunny body. Check yourself.

VARIATION:

Magnetic tape on the back of each hunter and bunny make it
fun. The game is good as a group instructional game, too.
This has been a real favorite of our children.

Peer teaching is an asset to any program.

TITLE: Sweet Treats

PURPOSE:
To develop the skill of listening for vowel digraph sounds in words.

MATERIALS:
Posterboard; candy jar and candy patterns (see Appendix A); felt-tipped markers; clear, self-adhesive plastic; scissors; 3" x 5" index cards; box and label for storage.

PREPARATION:
1. Trace two candy jar patterns on posterboard and label each one as shown below. Cover them with clear, self-adhesive plastic; then cut out each jar.

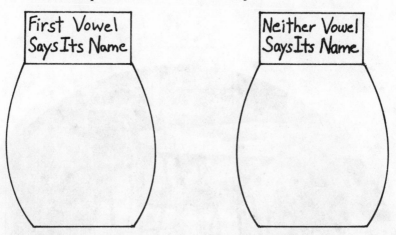

2. Trace 28 candy shapes on index cards and write the following words on them (one word per candy piece):

vein	oak	weigh	build
boat	sweet	leaf	their
goat	treat	wait	feather
fail	taught	beat	rain
earn	laugh	rail	bread
clean	show	again	team
toe	tail	coat	seed

3. Cover the index cards with clear, self-adhesive plastic; then cut out each candy piece. Be sure to code each candy piece on the back as a self-checking device. All candy pieces that fit into the first candy jar are coded number one and all pieces that belong in the second jar are coded number two.

4. Put candy jars and pieces in a box for storage and label your game.

DIRECTIONS TO THE CHILD:

All of the candy pieces fell out of their jars! See if you can put the right candy pieces back where they belong. Look at the word on each candy piece. Read the word and listen for the vowel sound. Each word has two vowels which walk together. When the first vowel says its own name, put the candy piece in jar number one. If neither vowel says its own name, put the candy piece in jar number two. Check the back of your candy pieces when you are done to see if you were right. Be careful not to get too hungry. Don't eat the candy!

TITLE: Trim the Hats

PURPOSE:
To practice and use the sounds associated with the vowel dipthongs oi, ay, au, aw, ow, ou.

MATERIALS:
Construction paper; posterboard; magnetic tape (optional); markers; scissors; hat and flower pattern (see Appendix A); clear, self-adhesive plastic; box and label for storage.

PREPARATION:
1. Trace six hats.
2. Fill in details. Mark each hat with au, aw, oi, ay, ow or ou.
3. Trace flowers (at least 4 for each hat) on different colors of construction paper.
4. Print a word which contains a vowel dipthong on each flower.
5. Cover hats and flowers with plastic before cutting out.
6. If it is available, cut strips of magnetic tape and attach to the hats and back of flowers.
7. Prepare a box and label for storage.

DIRECTIONS TO THE CHILD:
Trim the hats! Look at the letters on each hat and find the flowers which belong. When you are finished, read the words to someone.

VARIATION:
Different styles or types of hats can be used.

TITLE: Hoots for Home

PURPOSE:
To practice the long and short sounds of the double "o" (oo).

MATERIALS:
Posterboard (22" x 28" white or blue); markers (all colors); owl pattern (see Appendix A); scissors; magnetic tape (optional); clear, self-adhesive plastic; box and label for storage.

PREPARATION:
1. Cut the posterboard in half. Draw a tree on each half. Label o͞o and o͝o.
2. Color the trees with markers and cover with plastic.
3. Trace and color twelve owls. Use a light color such as yellow over the center part of the body.
4. Print a double "o" word on each owl. Suggested words are: long o͞o - food, moon, spoon, pool, hoot, stoop; short o͝o - hood, stood, wood, hook, cook, book.
5. Cover owls with plastic before cutting out.
6. Code backs of owls for self-checking.
7. If you have magnetic tape available, place several small pieces around the tree and in back of the owls.
8. Prepare a box and label for storage.

DIRECTIONS TO THE CHILD:
The little owls have come back to sleep. Help them to find their homes. Read the words on each owl. Put the owls in the tree which shows the sound you hear in a word. Look on the backs of owls to check yourself. Please do not hoot when you play this game.

VARIATIONS:
This game can be used either as an individual activity or as a group instructional game. If the children are advanced in phonetic skills or as they become so, words with variant spellings of the long and short "oo" sound can be added. For example: owls might be made with words such as could, would, should, shoe, true, and stew on them.

TITLE: Bag Some Peanuts

PURPOSE:
To practice the sound associated with the spellings ir, ur, and er.

MATERIALS:
Posterboard or index cards; elephant and peanut patterns (see Appendix A); markers; scissors; paste; clear, self-adhesive plastic; three small brown paper bags; box and label for storage.

PREPARATION:
1. Trace and color three circus elephants.
2. Label them ir, ur, er.
3. Cover each elephant with plastic, cut out, and paste each elephant to the side of a small paper bag. (A small milk carton could also be used.)
4. Trace and color at least 12 peanuts.
5. Print a word containing an ir, ur or er on each peanut. Suggested words are stir, her, bird, fur, curl, twirl, hurt, sir, herd, hurry, Bert, skirt.
6. Cover peanuts with plastic and cut out.
7. Prepare a box and label for storage.

DIRECTIONS TO THE CHILD:
Pretend you are going to feed the elephants at the circus. Look at the "name" on each elephant. Read and say the word on each peanut and give it to the correct elephant. Please don't get any peanut shells on the floor!

VARIATION:
More elephants containing variant spelling of the sound and peanuts with matching words can be added as children become more proficient. For example: or - word, work; ear - heard; etc.

TITLE: Knights in Shining Armor

PURPOSE:
To practice the use and pronunciation of the sounds associated
with kn, gn and wr.

MATERIALS:
Posterboard or index cards; knight, shield, and sword patterns
(see Appendix A); scissors; markers (all colors); razor blade;
clear, self-adhesive plastic; box and label for storage.

PREPARATION:
1. Trace at least six knights, shields, and swords on posterboard or index cards.

2. Fill in details with felt-tipped markers to your liking.

3. Each shield is given a letter combination of kn, gn or wr.
(Each combination should be used twice.)

4. Across each knight print a word such as knight, know,
gnat, gnaw, wring, write, eliminating the kn, gn or wr
and using a line in its place.

5. Print each word again in its complete form on a sword.

6. Cover knights, shields, and swords with plastic before
cutting out. With a razor blade cut a slit under each
knight's right hand.

7. Prepare a box and label for storage.

DIRECTIONS TO THE CHILD:
Look at the letter combination on each knight and place on
the knight a shield which will complete a word. Find the
matching sword word card and put it in the knight's hand.

12

Structural Analysis

TITLE: Plural Party

PURPOSE:
To reinforce the concept of changing "y" to "i" and adding "es" when spelling the plural form of certain nouns.

MATERIALS:
Sources for pictures; posterboard; marker (black); scissors; paste; clear, self-adhesive plastic; box and label for storage.

PREPARATION:
1. Find pictures to illustrate such words as party, baby, cherry, bunny, daddy, mommy, lady, strawberry, and candy.

2. Paste each picture on a 3" square of posterboard and print the singular form beneath the picture. Cover with plastic and cut out cards.

3. Print the plural form on the back of each card.

4. Prepare 3 sets of alphabet letters on 1" posterboard squares and make 10 extra sets of vowels.

5. Prepare a box and label for storage.

DIRECTIONS TO THE CHILD:
Find a friend and have a "Plural Party." Give each person the same number of cards. Look at the picture and word on each card. Use the letter cards and spell the plural for each word. Then check the back of the card and correct yourself.

VARIATION:
Pictures which represent other plural forms can be added to the game.

81

TITLE: Ghostly Guests

PURPOSE:

To practice the use of variant inflectional endings and verbs which double the final letters before ed, ing.

MATERIALS:

Index cards; double set of alphabet letters; ghost pattern (see Appendix A); scissors; clear, self-adhesive plastic; box and label for storage.

PREPARATION:

1. Trace ten ghosts. The index cards work well for this game.

2. Fill in facial features with a marker.

3. Print a word such as hop, tap, beg, pet, fit, tag, top, dab, tan, pat on each ghost. Cover with plastic and cut out.

4. On the back of each ghost print the same word using the "ed" and "ing" ending.

5. If you do not have them available, make a double set of alphabet letters and cut them apart.

6. Prepare a box and label for storage.

DIRECTIONS TO THE CHILD:

Ten ghosts have come to visit! Read the word on each ghost. Think about the rule for adding an ending to these words. Then spell out the ten words and add "ed" or "ing" to each. Check the back of the ghost to see if you are correct. If you made a mistake, respell the word correctly. Tell the ghosts not to haunt anyone!

VARIATION:

Holes can be punched into each ghost and letter card with a paper punch. The game can then become a pegboard learning center.

Also, the same sort of idea can be used for adjectives which change the "y" to "i" before adding er or est.

TITLE: Our Belongings

PURPOSE:
To practice the use of the 's and its meaning.

MATERIALS:
Children; share and tell items; camera and film; posterboard; glue; markers; box and label for storage.

PREPARATION:
1. Take photos of the children and articles that they bring for share and tell.
2. Mount photos on posterboard.
3. Print sentences on posterboard strips to match photos. *Do not* use the child's name but use a line where it should be.

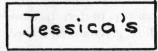

4. Print each child's name with an 's on a small strip of posterboard. It should fit over the straight line above.

Jessica's	Jeffrey's

5. Code the backs of photos, name cards, and sentence strips.
6. Prepare a box and label for storage.

DIRECTIONS TO THE CHILD:
Look at your friends and what belongs to them. Find a sentence and the person's name to complete it for each photo.

TITLE: Catch That Compound

PURPOSE:
To practice the recognition of compound words by matching
pictures and words.

MATERIALS:
Magazines and/or old workbooks; posterboard (two colors);
scissors; paste; thin-lined marker; clear, self-adhesive plastic;
box and label for storage.

PREPARATION:
1.   Find about 20 pictures which illustrate a compound word
      or draw your own.

2.   Measure 3" x 2" rectangles on posterboard. Mount the
      pictures, cover them with plastic, and cut out cards.
      Number the back of each card.

3.   Measure 1" x 3" strips on posterboard. Print the com-
      pound word for each picture on a strip with a thin-lined
      magic marker. Cover with plastic before cutting out.
      Number the back to correspond to a picture.

4.   Picture suggestions are: birdhouse, rowboat, airplane,
      policeman, grasshopper, treehouse, snowman, rooftop,
      corncob, grapefruit, ladybug, runway, footprints, cow-
      boy, firetruck, scarecrow, mailbox, greenhouse, school-
      house, raindrops.

5.   Prepare a box and label for storage.

DIRECTIONS TO THE CHILD:
Pick a friend to play this game with you. Each of you take
10 picture cards. Put the word cards in the center with the
words showing. Take turns finding the words to match your
pictures. Then turn the picture and word cards over and see
if you were right.

VARIATION:
Several children can play the game with the teacher. It can be
used as a diagnostic tool.

NOTE: We have devised several games dealing with the skill of
      compound words. Each one approaches the skill differ-
      ently or at a varying level of difficulty. This is our way of
      meeting individual needs. It also provides us with a vari-
      ety of materials for use in a learning center on this skill.

TITLE: Compound Fracture

PURPOSE:
To review or practice the concept of compound words.

MATERIALS:
Workbook or magazine pictures; scissors; paste; posterboard; clear, self-adhesive plastic; box and label for storage.

PREPARATION:
1. Find pictures of objects that when matched will make a compound word. Suggestions: a horse and a shoe, a nut and a shell, a tree and a house, a cow and a boy, etc.

2. Paste pictures on 3" x 4" posterboard rectangles, cover them with plastic, and cut them apart.

3. Make 1" x 3" name cards for each compound word that can be formed.

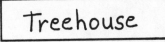

4. On the backs of cards code the two matching pictures and corresponding word card for self-checking.

5. Prepare a box and label for storage.

DIRECTIONS TO THE CHILD:
Look at each picture. Match two that will make a compound word. Put the word card for each word you make under the compound word that you make. Turn cards over to see if you are right.

VARIATION:
Use the game as a reading group activity. Give each child a picture card and have him team with another group member to form a compound word. An oral response can be given by another group member or it could be written on the chalkboard.

TITLE: Pancakeperson Compounds

PURPOSE:
To develop the skill of recognizing compound words.

MATERIALS:
Yellow posterboard; brown felt-tipped marker; scissors; list
of compound words; pancakeperson pattern (see Appendix
A); clear, self-adhesive plastic; box and label for storage.

PREPARATION:
1. Trace 12 pancakepersons onto yellow posterboard.

2. On one half of a pancakeperson, write the first part of a
    compound word, and the second part of the word on the
    other half.

3. Do the same for each pancakeperson, and cover all with
    plastic.

4. When you cut each pancakeperson in half, you make a
    puzzle out of each one. This is also a self-checking device.

5. Here is a list of compound words to use:

pancake	anything
mailbox	cannot
daylight	without
into	someone
bedroom	milkman
birthday	newspaper

6. Put all of the pancakeperson puzzles in a box for storage
    and label it.

DIRECTIONS TO THE CHILD:
The pancakepersons have lost half of their bodies! See if you
can find the other halves. When you put the puzzles together, you will make compound words. See if you can
put all of the pancakepersons back together! When you are
finished, read all of the compound words.

TITLE: Mend the Broken Hearts

PURPOSE:
To practice the use of compound words.

MATERIALS:
Red posterboard; heart-shaped pattern; magic markers; scissors; clear, self-adhesive plastic; box and label for storage.

PREPARATION:
1. Trace 10 to 12 hearts (4" wide) onto red posterboard.

2. Outline the heart with black magic marker and put a broken line down the center.

3. Write a word on each side of the heart which would form a compound word.

4. Cover with plastic; then cut out the hearts and cut along the broken line.

5. Prepare a box and label for storage.

DIRECTIONS TO THE CHILD:
Try to mend the broken hearts. Put the heart pieces together and read the compound words.

VARIATIONS:
Any outline can be used: trees for Christmas, shamrock for St. Patrick's Day, etc.

TITLE: A Dog's Life

PURPOSE:
To practice the concept of contractions.

MATERIALS:
Index cards (5" x 8") or posterboard; scissors; markers; dog and doghouse patterns (see Appendix A); clear, self-adhesive plastic; box for storage and a label.

PREPARATION:
1. Trace or draw ten dog and ten doghouse shapes.
2. Outline each and color in details.
3. Print a contraction on each dog and the words for these contractions on each doghouse.

4. Cover with plastic and cut out.
5. Code backs of dogs and doghouses for self-checking.
6. Prepare box and label for storage.

DIRECTIONS TO THE CHILD:
These little dogs need a home. Can you help each of them to find a good home? Match the contractions with words. Turn dogs and dog houses over to check yourself.

VARIATIONS:
We have enjoyed using this game as a group activity. By placing magnetic tape on the back of each piece, it becomes a useful game for a chalkboard or other magnetic surface.

TITLE: Lovebirds

PURPOSE:
To practice the concept of contractions.

MATERIALS:
Red and white posterboard; scissors; markers; bird shapes (see Appendix A); white construction paper; paste; clear, self-adhesive plastic; box and label for storage.

PREPARATION:
1. Draw eight to ten branches on white posterboard.

2. Color branches brown and print a contraction on each.

3. Trace eight to ten sets of lovebirds onto red posterboard.

4. Color facial features and hats.

5. Make little hearts from white construction paper.

6. Print the words for contractions on each of two hearts.

7. Paste the two hearts which form a contraction on the breasts of a set of birds.

8. Cover birds and branches with plastic. Cut out branches and cut each set of birds in half. Number sets on the back as a self-checking device.

9. Prepare a box and label for storage.

DIRECTIONS TO THE CHILD:
Read the two words on each set. Match the lovebirds. Look on the back to check yourself. Find the right branch for each set of birds.

VARIATIONS:
Any shapes which would make a likely pair could be used. Instead of contractions, compound words could be used or words for pairs such as cup/saucer, pencil/paper, etc.

TITLE: Monkey in the Tree

PURPOSE:
To develop the skill of identifying root words.

MATERIALS:
4" x 6" index cards; posterboard or cardboard; monkey and
tree patterns (see Appendix A); markers; clear, self-adhesive
plastic; scissors; magnetic tape; list of root words and their
variants; box and label for storage.

PREPARATION:
1.　Make a monkey pattern and trace forms on index cards.

2.　Write a root word on each monkey.

3.　Cover each monkey with clear, self-adhesive plastic before
　　cutting it out.

4.　Put magnetic tape on the back of each monkey.

5.　Draw trees with root word derivatives written on
　　each one. Cover with plastic before cutting out.

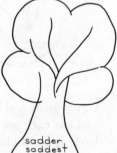

6.　Magnetize each of the trees.

7.　Prepare a box and label for storage.

DIRECTIONS TO THE CHILD:
Line up the trees and make a jungle. Put each monkey in the
right tree. Look for the root word you can see in the words
written on each tree.

VARIATIONS:
Contractions could be written on each monkey, and their long
forms could be written on the trees.

TITLE: Count the Syllables

PURPOSE:
To refine the skill of hearing the number of syllables in a word.

MATERIALS:
Posterboard (any color); scissors; paste; markers; pictures from old books or magazines; clear, self-adhesive plastic; box for storage and a label.

PREPARATION:
1. Find at least twelve pictures of 1, 2, 3, and 4 syllable words or draw them. Examples: fox, robin, anteater, caterpillar.

2. Measure 4" x 4" squares on posterboard. Mount pictures on squares, cover with plastic, and cut out.

3. Mark the number of syllables on the back of each card for self-checking.

4. Prepare box and label for storage.

DIRECTIONS TO THE CHILD:
Look at each picture. Say the word and think how many syllables it has. Look on the back of the card to check yourself.

VARIATIONS:
This game could be used as a part of a learning center on syllables, an instructional aid in a reading group, or a diagnostic check-up tool.

TITLE: Flying Syllables

PURPOSE:
To give the child practice in listening for and determining how many syllables are in a word.

MATERIALS:
5" x 8" index cards; felt-tipped markers; various colors of construction paper or posterboard; kite pattern (see Appendix A); scissors; list of multi-syllable words; clear, self-adhesive plastic; magnetic tape; box and label for storage.

PREPARATION:
1. Trace the kite pattern on a 5" x 8" index card. Make as many kites as you have words on your list. Write a multi-syllable word on each kite.

2. Cover kites with plastic before cutting out.

3. Code each kite on the back by writing the number of syllables contained in each word. Then magnetize with magnetic tape.

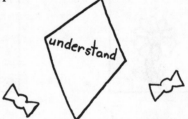

4. On the construction paper or the posterboard, draw small "ties" for the tails of each kite. Make a tail for every syllable in each word.

5. Cover tails with clear, self-adhesive plastic, cut out, and magnetize with magnetic tape.

6. Put in a storage box and label.

DIRECTIONS TO THE CHILD:
Take all the kites and put them on a magnetic surface. Read the word on a kite and put as many tails on it as there are syllables in the word. Look on the back of each kite to check yourself.

VARIATION:
Use the game for the auditory discrimination of syllables for children who are not yet ready to read the words and determine syllables but should begin to listen for word parts.

TITLE: Lurking Lions

PURPOSE:
To reinforce the skill of recognizing and using basic syllabication rules.

MATERIALS:
Pattern for lion (see Appendix A); 5 plastic fruit baskets (one-pint size); felt-tipped markers; 5" x 8" index cards; clear, self-adhesive plastic; scissors; large box for storage and a label.

PREPARATION:
1. Write each of these basic rules of syllabication on a 2" x 3" strip of index card:

   Rule 1   Single consonant between two vowels
   Rule 2   Double consonant between two vowels
   Rule 3   Consonant before final "le"
   Rule 4   Suffix "ed" is a separate syllable
   Rule 5   "ing" is usually a separate syllable

2. Number and label the plastic fruit baskets with these cards. These baskets will represent cages for the lions.

3. Trace 30 lion pattern shapes—each one on a 5" x 8" card.

4. On each lion write one of the following words. Each one fits into one of the rules of syllabication written on the cages.

1		2	
pupil	(pu pil)	letter	(let ter)
broken	(bro ken)	pressure	(pres sure)
mural	(mu ral)	happy	(hap py)
token	(to ken)	ribbon	(rib bon)
taken	(ta ken)	little	(lit tle)
		bigger	(big ger)
		rabbit	(rab bit)
		dessert	(des sert)

3		4	
able	(a ble)	planted	(plant ed)
table	(ta ble)	wanted	(want ed)
turtle	(tur tle)	molded	(mold ed)
circle	(cir cle)	needed	(need ed)
whistle	(whis tle)	folded	(fold ed)
maple	(ma ple)		

5

watching (watch ing)
seeing (see ing)
talking (talk ing)
walking (walk ing)
lurking (lurk ing)
smiling (smil ing)

5. Code each lion on the back with the syllabication rule number and the word breakdown in syllables.

6. Cover each lion with clear, self-adhesive plastic; then cut it out.

7. Put the lions and their "cages" in a box for storage and label your game.

DIRECTIONS TO THE CHILD:

The lions have escaped from the zoo! It's your job to find them and put them back into their proper cages. Sort out the cages. Read the rules on the front of each cage. Look at each lion and read the word written on his tummy. Figure out which rule you would use if you were breaking the lion's word into syllables. Look for a clue in each word. To help you figure out the right answers, read the word on the back of each lion; it is already broken down into syllables for you. Which rule did you use for each lion? You will find them on the cages. Put the lions back in their right cages and be sure not to let them bite you!

TITLE: Prefix Piggies

PURPOSE:
To practice the concept of a prefix and a root word.

MATERIALS:
Posterboard; scissors; markers; pig pattern (see Appendix A); clear, self-adhesive plastic; word list; box for storage and a label.

PREPARATION:
1. Make at least a dozen pig outlines on posterboard and fill in details.
2. Print a prefix on the head and a root word on the body before covering with plastic and cutting the head from the body! Suggested words are unhappy, display, redo, unkind, inside, ahead, disbelieve, unclear, replay, inhale, away, disagree.

3. Prepare a box and label for storage.

DIRECTIONS TO THE CHILD:
Don't lose your head! Put the Prefix Piggies together. Read each word that you make. Be sure to look at prefixes and root words.

VARIATIONS:
The prefix could stand alone on the head and the body could contain the meaning of the prefix. Any animal figure could be used, it's just that our children have a thing about pigs! They love them!

TITLE: Suffix Squirrel

PURPOSE:
To study and review the concept of the root word and suffix.

MATERIALS:
Posterboard; scissors; squirrel design (see Appendix A); word list; markers; clear, self-adhesive plastic; box for storage and a label.

PREPARATION:
1. Trace on posterboard ten to twelve squirrel designs. One or more colors of posterboard can be used.

2. After outlining the figures and filling in details, write a root word on each body and a suffix on each tail. Cover with plastic.

3. Cut out squirrels cutting each tail away from the body. Follow the rounded tail section rather than make the cut in jigsaw style.

4. Prepare a box and label for storage.

DIRECTIONS TO THE CHILD:
Give each squirrel a tail. Read each word that you make. Be sure not to lose your tails!

VARIATION:
Instead of using just the squirrel, several different animals and their tails could be used. Nuts could be added which give the meaning of the word or a sentence which uses the word.

TITLE: Rooty Ants

PURPOSE:
To reinforce the concepts of prefix, root word, and suffix.

MATERIALS:
Posterboard; ant pattern (see Appendix A); word list; scissors; magic marker (black); clear, self-adhesive plastic; box and label for storage.

PREPARATION:
1. Trace the outline of ten ants onto posterboard. Several colors could be used.

2. Outline the body parts.

3. Print a prefix on the head, a root word on the thorax, and a suffix on the abdomen. (This is a good way to review your knowledge of insects and that of the children, too!)

4. Cover with plastic; cut the head and abdomen away, and you've got a "Rooty Ant" puzzle!

5. Suggested words are: unthoughtful, unlikely, unkindly, disobeyed, replaying, impolitely, unfriendly, unfeeling, awaiting, unhealthy.

6. Be sure to space word parts on the puzzle pieces so that they are easy to recognize and unlock.

7. Prepare box and label for storage.

DIRECTIONS TO THE CHILD:
Look at the bodies of the ants. See if you can add a prefix and a suffix to each one. Make a whole ant for each body.

VARIATIONS:

This game can be used as the initial or review lesson on root words, prefixes, and suffixes. Magnetic tape on the backs of each piece would make it a fine magnetic board tool for use with an individual child or a reading skill group.

Don't forget the value of using the ants to discuss the meanings of prefixes and suffixes and how they can change the meaning of a root word.

Working independently enhances decision making.

Dictionary Skills

TITLE: Willie the Worm says: "Alphabetize Yourself!"

PURPOSE:
To develop the skill of alphabetizing.

MATERIALS:
Posterboard; markers; scissors; Willie the Worm pattern (see Appendix A); clear, self-adhesive plastic; box and label for storage of game; list of names of children in your class.

PREPARATION:
1.   Draw Willie the Worm.

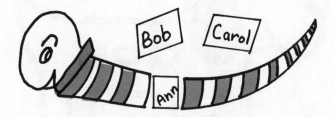

2.   On posterboard mark off enough rectangles (large enough to be used as Willie the Worm's middle segments) for each child in your class. Write the first names of the children in your class on these rectangles.

3.   Cover Willie the Worm and names with plastic before cutting out.

4.   Code the back of each rectangle numerically in alphabetical order as a self-checking device.

5.   Store Willie the Worm and his name card segments in a box and label.

DIRECTIONS TO THE CHILD:
Give Willie the Worm a body by putting the names in ABC order. Check the back of each card when you are done to see if they are in the right order.

VARIATION:
Use children's surnames as a follow-up game.

TITLE: Alphabet Doggies

PURPOSE:
To develop the skill of alphabetizing.

MATERIALS:
Posterboard; felt-tipped markers; scissors; list of words to be alphabetized; doggie pattern (see Appendix A); clear, self-adhesive plastic; box and label for storage.

PREPARATION:
1. Trace a dog shape on posterboard for each of the words on your list.
2. Write a word on each dog.

3. Cover each dog with self-adhesive plastic before cutting out.
4. For self-checking purposes, number each dog on the back as it would appear if in alphabetical order. Place dogs in a box and label it.

DIRECTIONS TO THE CHILD:
Put the doggies in alphabetical, or ABC, order. When you are finished, check your answers by looking on the back of each doggie.

VARIATIONS:

A more advanced step of alphabetizing can be added to this game. To differentiate between simple alphabetizing and more advanced alphabetizing, write words that must be alphabetized by their second and/or third letters on doggie dishes.

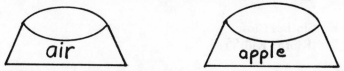

Children can feed the doggies once they've been put in ABC order. This game can also be used with a group of children. The doggies can be divided between two teams. The first team to get the doggies and dishes in proper ABC order wins.

TITLE: Clothes Closet
(Klōthz Klŏz′ĕt)

PURPOSE:
To practice the use of diacritical markings and pronunciation clues as found in the dictionary.

MATERIALS:
Old magazines and/or catalogs; posterboard; scissors; glue; markers (medium and fine-lined); clear, self-adhesive plastic; box and label for storage.

PREPARATION:
1. Find approximately twelve pictures of clothing which children like to wear.

2. Measure rectangles on posterboard. Mount each picture on a rectangle and print its name below. Example: sneakers.

3. Measure strips of posterboard, and on each strip print the word in parentheses as it would be pronounced. Example: (snēk′ẽrz).

4. Cover pictures and words with plastic before cutting out. On the backs, code each picture and matching word card for self-checking.

5. Prepare a box and label for storage.

DIRECTIONS TO THE CHILD:
Look at each picture. Say its name and look at the way it is spelled. Match each picture with a card which shows how that word would look in the pronunciation section of the dictionary. Turn pictures and word cards over to see if you are right.

TITLE: Diacritical Decisions

PURPOSE:
To practice the use of diacritical marks for long and short vowels.

MATERIALS:
Posterboard; old workbooks; scissors; marker (black); paste; clear, self-adhesive plastic; box and label for storage.

PREPARATION:
1. Find four pictures for each of the long and short vowel sounds.

2. Cut five pieces of posterboard, each 9" x 12".

3. Prepare a card for each vowel letter, drawing nine 3" squares. Label the top of each card using the macron and breve.

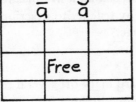

4. Paste the eight pictures on each card, leaving one space in the center free. Cover with plastic.

5. Draw three-inch square markers for each card using appropriate vowels and diacritical markings for each picture. Cover with plastic and cut out.

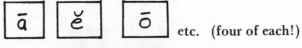 etc. (four of each!)

6. Prepare a box and label for storage.

DIRECTIONS TO THE CHILD:
Look at the pictures on each card. Say each name. Find a marker which matches the vowel sound you hear and cover a picture with it. Have someone check your work.

VARIATION:
This game can be used as a diagnostic tool or a reading group activity.

14

Comprehension

TITLE: Yummy in the Tummy!

PURPOSE:

To develop comprehension skills in using context clues, spelling skills, and word recognition.

MATERIALS:

Pictures of children's food favorites; posterboard; scissors; glue; markers; clear, self-adhesive plastic; index cards (3" x 5"); riddles composed by teacher to describe foods; box, envelope, and label for storage.

PREPARATION:

1. On posterboard mark off several rectangles. Mount food pictures (can be obtained from magazines and workbooks) on rectangles. Cover with plastic and cut up into cards.

2. Write labeling word on back of each card.

3. On 3" x 5" index cards write riddles to describe each food item and number each one. Cover with plastic. Write the answers on a key card.

Example:

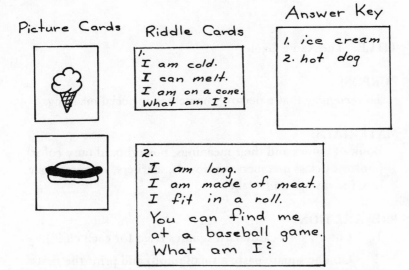

4. Make name cards to go with each picture. Cover with plastic before cutting out.

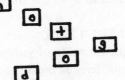

5. Make a duplicate set of word cards to describe the foods. Cover them with plastic and cut them into small letter blocks.

6. Store pictures, riddles, and word cards in a box. Put small letter blocks in an envelope or smaller box to help keep the small pieces together and store with other game parts.

DIRECTIONS TO THE CHILD:

Step 1. Read the riddles and match them with the pictures they describe. Check the answer key to see if you are correct.

Step 2. Match the picture cards with the word cards. Turn over picture cards to check yourself.

Step 3. Lay the picture cards on the table and, using the letter blocks, see if you can spell the words to describe each picture. Be careful not to eat any of the game parts!

VARIATIONS:

The picture cards and the riddle cards could be used as group games.

TITLE: The Name Game

PURPOSE:
To recognize that a person's name has a special meaning.

MATERIALS:
Book of names and their meanings, posterboard (any color), photos of class members (optional), markers, scissors, paste, box for storage and a label.

PREPARATION:
1. Cut 4" x 4" cardboard squares (two for each child).
2. On one square paste a small photo and print the first name of a child under it.
3. On another square print the meaning of the child's name. (Print the name on the other side for self-correction.)

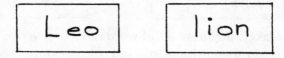

4. Prepare box and label for storage.

DIRECTIONS TO THE CHILD:
Do you know the meaning of your name? Do you know what the names of your friends mean? See if you can match a name with a meaning. Check yourself.

VARIATIONS:
Use the same technique with the picture of familiar animals and match with the name meanings. This game can be successfully used with small groups as well as individually.

TITLE: Match the Horses

PURPOSE:
To develop comprehension skills in reading.

MATERIALS:
Pictures of various kinds of horses (real or inanimate) which can be obtained from workbooks, magazines, or a beginning book about horses; posterboard; glue; scissors; 3" x 5" index cards; markers; clear, self-adhesive plastic; box and label for storage.

PREPARATION:
1. Cut out pictures of horses and mount each one on poster-board. Cover with plastic and cut up into cards.

2. Write a brief description of each horse on a 3" x 5" index card. Please note distinguishing characteristics of each horse.

3. Cover index cards, after writing descriptions, with clear, self-adhesive plastic.

4. Code each picture and corresponding description on the back of cards as a self-checking device.

5. Store component game parts in a small box or plastic container.

DIRECTIONS TO THE CHILD:
Match each horse with the sentences that tell about that horse. Check your answers on the back of each picture and card to see if you are correct. Be careful not to let any of the horses gallop away from you!

VARIATIONS:
Other animals could be used as the subject matter for this game: cats, dogs, snakes, etc., depending upon the interest and reading levels of the children you have. This particular game was a favorite among horse lovers!

TITLE: Nursery Rhyme Jumble

PURPOSE:
To develop the comprehension skill of arranging story parts in sequential order.

MATERIALS:
Nursery rhymes; typewriter (optional); posterboard in several colors; felt-tipped markers; scissors; glue; clear, self-adhesive plastic; index cards; box and label for storage.

PREPARATION:
1.   Type a nursery rhyme with a primary typewriter or print on several index cards.

2.   Mount the cards to one nursery rhyme on one color of posterboard and cover with clear, self-adhesive plastic. This is done to help the child keep the appropriate nursery rhymes together. Do the same for each nursery rhyme, remembering to mount each group of cards on a different color.

3.   Code the mounted cards by writing numbers on the back. Use a complete sequence of numbers for each nursery rhyme. The child can use this as a self-checking device.

4.   After all nursery rhymes are printed, mounted, and covered with clear self-adhesive plastic, store in a box and label it.

DIRECTIONS TO THE CHILD:
Take out all of the cards in the box. Put all red cards together, all blue cards together, all green cards together, and so on. Each group of cards has a nursery rhyme written on it, but they are not in order. You must read each story part and put them in the right order. Check your answers on the back of each card when you are done.

VARIATIONS:
Any stories will do to give variety. More games of this nature can be made as a sequel to the nursery rhymes.

Part IV
CONTENT-ORIENTED READING GAMES

15

Creative Writing

TITLE: Play Ball!

PURPOSE:
To extend the use of language skills through creative writing.

MATERIALS:
Posterboard (white); index cards (4" x 6"); felt-tipped markers;
clear, self-adhesive plastic; scissors; list of story starters; pattern for baseball player, baseball, and mitt (see Appendix A);
box and label for storage.

PREPARATION:
1. Trace the shape of the baseball player pattern on white
    posterboard and color it with felt-tipped markers.

2. Trace the baseball pattern on index cards to make as
    many baseballs as you need for your story starters. Cover
    player and baseballs with plastic and cut out.

3. On the back of each baseball write a story starter.

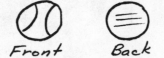

Front   Back

4. Make a baseball mitt from the pattern to go with each
    baseball. Cover with plastic and cut out. Cut a slot in
    each baseball mitt. Place a baseball in each mitt.

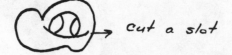

cut a slot

5. Here are some story starters:

    a. What would you do if you lived next door to a
        monster?

    b. What would you do if you lived during the time of
        the dinosaurs? Write your story.

    c. What would it be like if you were as small as your
        thumb? What would you be able to do?

d. Imagine that you have an alligator as a pet. Wri
your story.

e. Imagine that you got stuck inside a gigantic ice
cream cone. How would it feel? Describe your re-
action.

6. Prepare a box and label for storage.

DIRECTIONS TO THE CHILD:

Pick a baseball and read the story starter written on the back
of it. After you read it, write your story. Don't strike out!
Read your finished story to a friend.

VARIATION:

This activity could be displayed on a bulletin board by using
the baseball player as the main character. Arrange the base-
balls and mitts around the baseball player. Post your directions along with the display.

TITLE: Animal Talk

PURPOSE:
To interpret facial expressions of animals in order to create imaginative stories.

MATERIALS:
Old calendars, magazines, or greeting cards; posterboard; scissors; paste; marker; clear, self-adhesive plastic; box and label for storage.

PREPARATION:
1. Find expressive pictures of animals.

2. On posterboard measure several rectangles. Mount the pictures on the rectangles, leaving enough room to print captions and/or starter questions to spark ideas. Cover with plastic before cutting up into cards.

3. Some examples are:

    a. A cat and a dog cuddled together:

        Caption: Love

        Starter: In your story use some of these words: cute, love, pals, puppy, friends, adorable, kitten.

    b. A group of dogs with mouths open:

        Caption: A new singing group in town!

        Starter: What do they call themselves? Write a story about the latest "rock'n roll" group!

    c. Two cats, one with eyes closed, one with mouth open:

        Caption: A surprise? A scare?

        Starter: What do you see? What do they see? Tell about the picture.

    d. Two animals looking closely at one another:

        Caption: Oh, my!

        Starter: Here is trouble! Write a story to tell us about it.

e. A little kitten with eyes tightly closed:

Caption: Here is a little kitten.

Starter: Is the kitten sad? Is the kitten sleepy? Is the kitten dreaming? Write a story about the little kitten.

4. Prepare a box and label for storage.

DIRECTIONS TO THE CHILD:
If these animals could talk what would they say? Find a picture that you really like and write a story about it.

Interest in reading determines success.

TITLE: Raggedy Rita's Story Garden

PURPOSE:

To extend a child's language skills through creative writing expression.

MATERIALS:

Red, green, and white posterboard; felt-tipped markers; rag doll and "heart flower" patterns (see Appendix A); scissors; clear, self-adhesive plastic; list of creative writing story starters; box and label for storage.

PREPARATION:

1. Draw a rag doll figure on white posterboard and color it in with felt-tipped markers. Cover with plastic and cut out.

2. Draw on red posterboard as many "heart flowers" as are needed for your story starters. Number each heart on the front. This is done to identify the story starter the child used to write his story. Cover with plastic and cut out. Then write a story starter on the back of each heart.

3. Draw the stem and petals on green posterboard. Make one to match each heart. Cover with plastic and cut out. These will be used as holders for the hearts.

4.   You may wish to display the "heart flowers" on a bulletin board with the rag doll as a display. By stapling the petal holder onto a bulletin board, you will provide a pocket for the story starter heart.

staples

5.   Here are some examples of story starters to use:

   a.   If you could have three wishes come true, what would they be?

   b.   Pretend you are a giant. Tell your story.

   c.   What if everything in the world turned red?

   d.   What if we went to school at night instead of days? How would your life be different?

   e.   Pretend you are a midget. Tell your story.

6.   Prepare box and label for storage.

DIRECTIONS TO THE CHILD:

Pick a heart flower from Raggedy Rita's garden. On a piece of paper write a story about the idea on the back of each heart. At the top of the paper write the number of the story starter. Draw a picture to go with your story if you wish.

Photo Courtesy—National Education Association Publishing Joe Di Dio

16
Literature

TITLE: Color Fun at Pooh Corner

PURPOSE:
To practice color recognition and following directions.

MATERIALS:
The Pooh Party Book by Virginia Ellison, E. P. Dutton, 1971;
posterboard or felt pieces; markers (all colors); scissors; index
cards (3" x 5"); clear, self-adhesive plastic; box and label for
storage.

PREPARATION:
1. Trace the Pooh characters from the section "Pooh and
    His Friends for Tracing," pg. 138-145, The Pooh Party
    Book onto posterboard or felt.

2. If you use posterboard, color figures with magic marker.
    Cover with plastic before cutting out.

3. Make a different color object for each character below
    from felt or posterboard. If you use posterboard, cover
    with plastic before cutting out.

    Christopher Robin—an orange carrot
    Pooh—a yellow flower
    Piglet—a red shirt
    Kanga—a green apron
    Baby Roo—a blue balloon
    Eeyore—a red bow
    Owl—a purple rug

4. Now, print a set of directions on index cards for each
    character and object. Cover cards with plastic.

    a. Christopher Robin wants to eat an orange carrot.
        Please give him one.

    b. Kanga must make dinner for little Roo. Find her
        green apron and put it on her.

    c. Piglet wants to go out to play. Dress him in his
        little red shirt.

d.   Piglet found Baby Roo's blue balloon. Please give it to Baby Roo.

e.   Eeyore lost his red bow. Please help him to find it and put it on his tail.

f.   Pooh has picked a yellow flower. Please put it in his hand.

g.   Owl needs a purple rug. Can you get one for him?

5.   Prepare box and label for storage.

DIRECTIONS TO THE CHILD:

1.   (For an adult or child reader and a non-reading child) I am going to give you Pooh and his friends. I'm going to tell you to do something for each of them. Listen carefully and see if you can follow my directions.

2.   (For beginning readers who can play independently) Here are Pooh and his friends. Read each card and do what it tells you. Have someone check your game.

VARIATION:

Rather than a set of characters from one story, use a variety of the children's favorites. Other types of directions could be given.

TITLE: Guess Who Is Here?

PURPOSE:
To recognize names and pictures of favorite storybook friends.

MATERIALS:
Old magazines, catalogs, stickers; posterboard; scissors; paste; markers; clear, self-adhesive plastic; box and label for storage.

PREPARATION:
1. Find pictures of favorite storybook friends. Good sources are magazine advertisements, store catalogs, and sticker pictures made by some greeting card companies.

2. On posterboard measure several rectangles. You'll have to determine the size based on the pictures that you find. Mount pictures, cover with plastic, and cut into picture cards.

3. Measure strips of posterboard and print a character's name on each strip. Cover with plastic before cutting.

4. Make up simple riddles giving a clue to the identity of the storybook characters. Print or type these riddles onto posterboard rectangles. Cover with plastic and cut into cards.

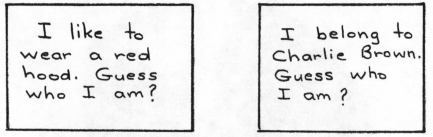

5. On backs of picture cards, name cards, and riddle cards code matching sets for self-checking.

6. Prepare a box and label for storage.

DIRECTIONS TO THE CHILD:
Some favorite storybook friends have come to visit. Read each riddle card. Find the picture and name card to match it. Check yourself by turning the cards over. Say hello to Snow White for me when you find her!

17
Mathematics

SKILL:
Word Recognition

TITLE: Shopping for Toys

PURPOSE:
To practice reading price tags, counting money, and making change.

MATERIALS:
A shoebox full of toys; price tags; colorful adhesive paper; scissors; a can of small change; thin-lined marker; labels.

PREPARATION:

1. Take yourself on an expedition to a few toy counters. Find some small packaged 5 and 10 cent items. Yes, if you look hard enough there are still a few to be found!

2. Buy some packages of small price tags.

3. Tag each toy by marking the number symbol for the price on one side and the price words on the other side. Place the toys in a shoebox.

4. A coffee can covered with colorful adhesive paper serves as a good money container.

5. Now comes the most difficult part! Collect your small change and place it in the can so that the children can handle true coins when playing the game.

6. Label shoebox and can and store together.

DIRECTIONS TO THE CHILD:

Find a toy that you would like to buy. Use the money from the can to pay for it. Be sure to read the price tag on the toy. Then you be the storekeeper and let someone else buy the toy.

VARIATION:

This game is best played by a teacher with a small group of children as an instructional aid. Children can take turns being storekeepers and customers. Food models, etc., could be used.

TITLE: Buy a Toy

PURPOSE:
To practice or follow-up work with money values, a dollar
and more.

MATERIALS:
Toy catalog and math workbooks; posterboard; scissors; paste;
markers; clear, self-adhesive plastic; box and label for storage.

PREPARATION:
1. Cut out 10 or 12 pictures of favorite or popular toys.

2. Mount them on 4" squares of posterboard.

3. Below picture print a cost on each square in two ways:

   $1.35

   One dollar and thirty-five cents

   Cover with plastic and cut out squares.

4. Old math workbooks which have actual reproductions of
   the coins can be used to find coins whose value will match
   the toy prices.

5. Mount these on 4" squares. Cover with plastic and cut
   up into cards.

6. Print the values on the back of each coin card as suggested in #3.

7. Prepare a box and label for storage.

DIRECTIONS TO THE CHILD:
Pretend you are buying a few of your favorite toys. See if
you can match a coin card with each toy and its price. Check
yourself!

VARIATION:
A hole can be punched into the top of each card for use on a
pegboard. You can purchase pieces of masonite pegboard at a
local building supply company. Mount it on a wooden base
and you can have a learning station. Title it "Match Board"
and place the pegs parallel to each other.

TITLE: Abbreviation Bunnies

PURPOSE:
To practice abbreviations for measurement words.

MATERIALS:
White posterboard; scissors; markers; bunny and carrot patterns (see Appendix A); clear, self-adhesive plastic; list of words and abbreviations; box for storage and label.

PREPARATION:
1. Make fourteen bunny outlines and fourteen carrot outlines on posterboard.

2. Fill in details.

3. Print a word on each bunny and its abbreviation on each carrot. Words and abbreviations which can be used are: day (da.), week (wk.), year (yr.), month (mo.), foot (ft.), inch (in.), yard (yd.), hour (hr.), minute (min.), pound (lb.), ounce (oz.), second (sec.), pint (pt.), quart (qt.).

4. Cover bunnies and carrots with plastic before cutting out. Cut around the paws of the bunnies so that a carrot can be slipped through with ease.

5. Code the bunnies and carrots as a self-checking device.

6. Prepare box and label for storage.

DIRECTIONS TO THE CHILD:

Feed each bunny a carrot. Find the carrot which belongs to each bunny. Read each word and practice its abbreviation. Turn them over to check yourself.

VARIATIONS:

An Easter egg can be used in place of a carrot as well as other animals and their favorite foods. Metric measurement abbreviations would make an interesting game.

Quality is a by-product of meaningful activities.

TITLE: Metric Mice

PURPOSE:

To practice the names of metric measurements and their abbreviations.

MATERIALS:

White posterboard or index cards; mouse and cheese patterns (see Appendix A); felt-tipped markers; list of metric measurement terms; clear, self-adhesive plastic; scissors; box and label for storage.

PREPARATION:

1. Trace the shape of ten mice and ten pieces of cheese on posterboard or index cards.

2. Fill in features of the mice with felt-tipped markers and color the cheese yellow. Outline mice and cheese with black.

3. Print a metric measurement term on each mouse and its abbreviation on a piece of cheese. Suggestions are gram (gr.), meter (m.), milligram (mg.), centimeter (cm.), milliliter (ml.), liter (l.), decimeter (dm.), millimeter (mm.), kilometer (km.), kilogram (kg.).

4. Cover mice and cheese with plastic before cutting out.

5. Code the mice and the cheese pieces as a self-checking device.

6. Prepare a box and label for storage.

DIRECTIONS TO THE CHILD:

The poor little mice have lost their cheese! Help each mouse to find its piece. Read the metric word on each mouse first and then find the correct abbreviation for each one on a piece of cheese. Turn the pieces over to check yourself. Remember— don't let the mice get away!

VARIATION:

Instead of words and abbreviations, equivalent measurements could be used and matched.

A happy, relaxed atmosphere is conducive to learning.

TITLE: Play the Centimeter Game

PURPOSE:
To practice measuring in centimeters and reading vocabulary words using metric terminology.

MATERIALS:
Old magazines or workbooks; posterboard; thin-lined markers; scissors; paste; clear, self-adhesive plastic; decimeter pattern (see Appendix A); box and label for storage.

PREPARATION:
1. Trace at least two decimeter rules.

10 centimeters = 1 decimeter

Fill in details, cover with plastic, and cut out.

2. Now, find at least ten small pictures which can be measured in centimeters. (Have a variety ranging from 1 to 10 centimeters in length.)

3. On posterboard mark off ten or more rectangles with dimensions of 6 centimeters x 10 centimeters. Mount pictures, cover with plastic, and cut out.

4. Print the correct measurement on the back of the card.

5. Print the answers on posterboard marked off into strips which measure 3 centimeters by 7 centimeters. Cover with plastic and cut up into answer cards.

6. Prepare a box and label for storage.

DIRECTIONS TO THE CHILD:
Have some fun with centimeters! Take a rule from the box and measure each picture. Put the right answer card under each picture. When you have measured each picture, turn the pictures over and check yourself.

VARIATIONS:
Have the children use the rule and measure objects in the room. The names of the objects can be listed and the measurement recorded. Also, the centimeter abbreviation can be added to each answer card.

TITLE: Metric Measure Up

PURPOSE:
To read and solve problems based upon the metric system of measurement.

MATERIALS:
Posterboard; thin-lined marker; old magazine or workbook; scissors; paste; clear, self-adhesive plastic; box and label for storage.

PREPARATION:
1. Draw at least five 4½" circles.

2. Find some small clever pictures to paste on each circle to make them more appealing and eye-catching.

3. Print a problem on each circle, such as:

   a. Get 5 people together. Mark off 5 meters on the playground. Have a race!

   b. Find something in the room that measures at least 3 meters.

   c. Make a picture of something that is 10 centimeters long.

   d. Take brown paper. Make a Jolly Green Giant who is 1 meter tall.

   e. Measure yourself in centimeters. Go to the wall chart. Mark how tall you are in centimeters next to your name.

4. Cover with plastic; cut out circles; prepare box and label.

5. Prepare a box and label for storage.

DIRECTIONS TO THE CHILD:
How well can you measure in meters? Try your skill with these problems.

VARIATIONS:
Results can be recorded on paper or discussed during a group activity. The game could be used as an instructional group activity rather than as an independent learning activity. Other problems using grams and liters can be devised as separate activities or added to the linear measurements as a potpourri of metric system problems. This game will also be a learning activity for teachers in America as we "bone up" on our metric rules!

TITLE: Birds Fly

PURPOSE:
To practice reading the words for the ordinal numbers concept.

MATERIALS:
Posterboard (two colors); old magazines or workbooks; felt-tipped markers; scissors; paste; clear, self-adhesive plastic; envelope and label for storage.

PREPARATION:
1. Cut a piece of posterboard 10" x 20". Title it "Birds Fly."

2. Find ten little pictures of birds flying in the same direction.

3. Paste the pictures across the center of the posterboard. Cover with plastic.

4. Mark off ten word cards 1" x 4" on another color posterboard. On each card write one of the first ten ordinals: first, second, third, etc. Cover with plastic and cut into cards.

5. Prepare an envelope and label for storage.

DIRECTIONS TO THE CHILD:
Help the birds to fly away! Put a word card under each bird to show in what order they are flying.

VARIATIONS:
Pictures of children, inanimate objects, or other animals could be used in place of birds. Another variation would be to write the ordinal words on the board and mount each picture on a separate card marked 1st, 2nd, etc. Children could then match the picture and its abbreviation with the appropriate word.

18

Science

TITLE: Insect Quiz

PURPOSE:
To practice the skill of classifying insects vs. non-insects and the skill of matching words with pictures.

MATERIALS:
Drawings or pictures of insects and non-insects; posterboard; jar rings; felt-tipped marker; scissors; paste; clear, self-adhesive plastic; box and label for storage of jar rings and word cards.

PREPARATION:
1. Use a whole piece of posterboard or a 15" x 24" piece. Title it "Insect Quiz."
2. Paste pictures of insects and non-insects randomly over the posterboard making sure that there is enough space for a jar ring to fit around a picture without interfering with another picture. Cover with plastic.
3. Make plastic-covered word cards with the name of each insect pictured.
4. Print the directions on the back of the posterboard.
5. Prepare a box for the storage of jar rings and word cards. You will need a jar ring for each non-insect. A small diagram of correct responses can also be included for self-checking.

DIRECTIONS TO THE CHILD:
Put a jar ring over the picture of every animal that is not an insect. Then put the name card for each insect over its picture.

VARIATIONS:
The game could be used by one child, a team of two, or a small group. Other science classifications could be used instead of insects. For example: living and non-living things, plants and animals, fruits and vegetables, reptiles and fish.

TITLE: Spring Flower Match

PURPOSE:

To learn to recognize that certain flowers are associated with the seasons and to practice reading the flower names.

MATERIALS:

Flower catalog or old magazines; posterboard; scissors; paste; felt-tipped marker; clear, self-adhesive plastic; box and label for storage.

PREPARATION:

1. Search through catalogs and magazines to find pictures of spring flowers. Possibilities are the pansy, iris, tulip, Easter lily, crocus, daffodil and lily-of-the valley.

2. Mark off 3½" squares on posterboard. Paste pictures on squares, cover with plastic, and cut out.

3. Mark off 1" x 3½" strips on posterboard. Print a flower name on each strip, cover with plastic, and cut out.

4. Prepare a box and label for storage.

5. Code the pictures and word cards by design or number for self-checking.

DIRECTIONS TO THE CHILD:

Spring has sprung! How many flowers do you know? Match the pictures with the word cards. Check yourself.

VARIATIONS:

Naturally, the same idea would be effective for the other seasons. Such games could be a part of a learning center based on the seasons of the year.

TITLE: Animal Babies

PURPOSE:
To learn the correct names of familiar animal babies and match names with pictures.

MATERIALS:
Old magazines or workbooks; posterboard; scissors; paste; felt-tipped marker; clear, self-adhesive plastic; box and label for storage.

PREPARATION:
1. Find as many pictures of animal babies as possible.

2. Mark off 4" x 4" squares on posterboard. Mount pictures on squares, cover with plastic, and cut out.

3. Mark off 1" x 3" strips on posterboard. Print the name of an animal baby on each strip, cover with plastic, and cut out.

4. Suggestions for babies are: cygnet (swan), kitten (cat), bunny or kitten (rabbit), puppy (dog), calf (cow), calf (elephant), nestling (bird), duckling (duck), fawn (deer), foal (horse), cub (bear), cub (lion).

5. Code the backs of pictures and word cards for self-checking.

6. Prepare a box and label for storage.

DIRECTIONS TO THE CHILD:
Name the babies! Match the word for each baby with its picture. Don't pet the babies. Their mothers might be watching. Look on the backs of pictures and word cards to see if you are right.

VARIATIONS:
Pictures of babies and mothers could be matched and word cards placed under pictures such as: fawn and doe, cub and lioness, etc.

131

TITLE: Rock Hunt

PURPOSE:
To match rock samples with the names and classification of rocks.

MATERIALS:
Posterboard; cement glue; felt-tipped marker; rock samples; scissors; box and label for storage.

PREPARATION:
1. Cut 3" x 3" squares of posterboard for each rock sample you have found or collected.

2. Cement each sample onto posterboard.

3. Print the name of each sample on 1" x 3" strips.

4. Cut three 2½" x 3" posterboard pieces. Make three labels— Igneous Rocks, Sedimentary Rocks, and Metamorphic Rocks.

5. Code sample cards and labels.

6. Store in a labeled box.

DIRECTIONS TO THE CHILD:
See what kind of a "Rock Hunter" you are. Match the rocks and their names. Then, see if you can classify them according to igneous, sedimentary, and metamorphic rocks.

VARIATION:
If you do not have rock samples available, pictures mounted on posterboard would be as effective. Or you could match samples with pictures of rocks.

TITLE: Dinosaurs at Dinnertime

PURPOSE:
To classify, match, and read about dinosaurs.

MATERIALS:
Plastic models of dinosaurs or pictures; reference materials on
dinosaurs; posterboard (two colors); index cards; scissors; felt-
tipped markers (wide and thin-lined); clear, self-adhesive plastic; box and label for storage.

PREPARATION:
1. Packages of dinosaur models are available at most toy
   stores.

2. Using two different colors, make two 4" x 5" labels
   which read "Meat-Eaters" and "Plant-Eaters. (Use the
   wide-tipped marker for labeling.) Cover with plastic.

3. Search the reference materials for a few facts about each
   of the dinosaurs you have represented (the meaning of
   its name, size, what it ate) and print the information on
   index cards.

4. These cards should then be mounted on posterboard.
   Correspond the information on plant-eaters to the color
   of the label for "Plant-Eaters" and the same for "Meat-
   Eaters." Cover with plastic and cut into cards.

5. Make name labels for each dinosaur model or picture
   again using the color code for "Meat-Eaters" and "Plant-
   Eaters."

6. Now you have a self-checking device as well as a self-
   learning type of game.

7. Prepare a box and label for storage.

DIRECTIONS TO THE CHILD:
How much do you know about dinosaurs? Try this game in
three steps:
1. Name the dinosaurs.

2. Classify them according to "Meat-Eaters" and
   "Plant-Eaters."

3. Find the card which tells you about each dinosaur
   and match it to the model.

Now, find a friend and ask him or her some questions about dinosaurs. Play the game together.

VARIATION:

Models of other animals, plants, or objects could be used. Use something that is of particular interest to your children (kinds of model cards, dolls, farm animals, furniture, clocks, etc.).

19

Social Studies

TITLE: Which Worker Am I?

PURPOSE:
To develop reading comprehension skills.

MATERIALS:
Pictures of workers in various occupations; posterboard; index cards (3" x 5"); clear, self-adhesive plastic; scissors; glue; felt-tipped markers; box and label for storage.

PREPARATION:
1. Cut out pictures of people in various occupations. Mount these pictures on posterboard; cover with clear, self-adhesive plastic; and cut them out.

2. Using index cards, write a description consisting of one sentence to accompany each picture. A description could also be given in paragraph form.

3. Mount the index cards on posterboard to make them more attractive. Cover them with clear, self-adhesive plastic; and cut into cards.

4. Write the names of workers on 2" x 4" strips of poster-board.

5. Code all game parts on the back of cards as a self-checking device.

6. Place pictures, descriptions, and name cards in a box and label it.

DIRECTIONS TO THE CHILD:
Sort all of the pictures and lay them out on the table. Read the sentence cards. Find the picture to go with each description. When you are finished, match the name cards with their pictures.

TITLE: Hornbook

PURPOSE:
To learn about life in early America and practice comprehension and study skills at the same time.

MATERIALS:
Posterboard; hornbook pattern; scissors; glue; clear, self-adhesive plastic; old magazines and/or catalogs; box and label for storage.

PREPARATION:
1. Find pictures of objects which are representative of early America—tools, furniture, articles of clothing, etc.

2. Mount and label each picture onto pieces of posterboard cut out in the form of hornbooks. Cover the picture with clear adhesive to resemble the horn used in early days.

3. On the other side of the posterboard print questions or directions such as:

    (a) How was this tool used? Look up the information in the dictionary or encyclopedia.

    (b) Of what material is this dress probably made? How do you know? Where can you find out?

    (c) This piece of furniture was used for many purposes. Can you find out what they were?

4. Prepare a box and label for storage.

DIRECTIONS TO THE CHILD:
See how much you know or can find out about early America. Play this game by yourself or with a friend. You may go to the library to find information. You may also want to share the information with others by telling or writing stories.

VARIATIONS:
This game lends itself to a learning center format. It can be used as a review or as a motivating activity for a study of early American life.

20
Spelling

SKILLS:
Alphabetizing
Phonetic Analysis
Structural Analysis

TITLE: Spell My Name

PURPOSE:
To develop skill in alphabetizing and spelling animal names.

MATERIALS:
Pictures of animals (domestic and wild) taken from magazines or workbooks; posterboard; glue; scissors; markers; clear, self-adhesive plastic; box and label for storage.

PREPARATION:
1. Cut out pictures of animals—one for each letter of the alphabet.
2. Mark off squares on posterboard; mount pictures on squares; cover with plastic before cutting.
3. On the back of each card write the correct spelling of each animal name.
4. Numerate the cards on the back as they would appear in alphabetical sequence as a self-checking device.
5. Prepare box and label for storage.

DIRECTIONS TO THE CHILD:
Step 1: Look at each of the animal pictures and say the name to yourself. Then put the animals in ABC order. Check the back of each card to see if you are correct.

Step 2: Look at each of the animal pictures and say their names. On a piece of paper write in a column a number for each animal card. Write the animal name next to each number on your paper. Check your spelling with the name on the back of each card.

TITLE: Spell Time

PURPOSE:
To strengthen phonics skills and give practice in spelling.

MATERIALS:
3" x 5" index cards; list of simple words from child's reading vocabulary; markers; clear, self-adhesive plastic; three-dimensional letters made of plastic or pressed cardboard; box and label for storage.

PREPARATION:
1. Write words on index cards. Cover with plastic.
2. Include a corresponding three-dimensional letter for every letter on each word card.
3. Store cards and letters in a labeled box.

DIRECTIONS TO THE CHILD:
Find the letters to spell the word on each card.

VARIATIONS:
For developing readiness skills entitle the game "Letter Match Up" and use only letter cards instead of word cards. The child must then match the three-dimensional letter with the letter card.

NOTE: For the child with perceptual problems the letter should be placed right on top of the written letter on the card.

For a group game, place the plastic letters in a box or container in the middle of a table. Players may range from 2 to 6 in number. Deal a word card to each child (2 or 3 cards per child for a longer game). Children take turns in feeling-drawing for a letter from the container to match up with one of the letters in their word. The first child to completely spell his word is the winner.

Secrets for Success

There are no quick and easy answers to the education of children. We have found success in the use of our reading games because of a variety of reasons.

We believe that if we are going to give children a quality education, then quality must begin with the teacher and what he or she presents to children. Quality is a by-product that results from introducing "caring" into teaching; caring enough to incorporate a child's interests into classroom instruction and to produce a game that is well-made, meets a child's instructional needs, and is fun to play. A game is much more meaningful to a child if his or her favorite animal is used as a basis of the skill and drill, and it says to a child: "My teacher cares for me." Also, if we expect children to strive for quality, then we must set the example.

By making a game when needed to introduce or extend a skill, a fine collection begins to accumulate over a period of months. It does not happen overnight. Many of the games we have developed can be made in a relatively short amount of time while many others take a longer time to complete. If you find that you are unable to spend all of the time you need to make games, here is the perfect way to involve parents in your program. Approach them and ask for help.

Another factor in achieving success is teaching children how to use the games from the inception of the program. And games can be used anywhere in the room or the building as long as they are returned to the storage area.

We initially developed many of the games as learning centers and later adapted them into game forms when a child was ready for the skill. Other games were used as a part of small group instruction and were later adapted for individual use in the classroom.

Our games are based upon a skill sequence and can be used with any basic reading program. They can also be used on their own, in conjunction with an individualized reading program, and with a language-experience approach. Most reading skills in an elementary reading program are covered in our game collection. They are geared to the interest level of children approximately five to eight years of age or kindergarten through grade three. However, by merely changing the interest level, our games are adaptable to intermediate age children needing the basic reading skills. Most of the games provide instant feedback because of self-correction. Others serve as a diagnostic tool.

We found children off in corners or in our production room making games to add to the classroom collection. Many days children brought in games which they had made at home. There was a genuine interest on the part of several children to make games for others who were studying a particular skill with which they were familiar.

A sign-out system was developed when children began asking to take games home overnight and weekends to share with members of the family. This response helped to strengthen the tie between home and school.

Games are fun, and they turn children and teachers on to learning. They provide us with the special opportunity to use our children's interests and personalities in a meaningful learning scheme.

Finally, as you plan your program for child-centered activities, please keep in mind that a happy, relaxed atmosphere is conducive to learning. By giving children freedom to learn and, at the same time, instilling responsibility, an individual child's learning style is developed. A love of reading paves the way to a love of learning. The two are inseparable. Good luck to you as you prepare a learning climate which encourages "reading with a smile"!

APPENDIX A:
Patterns for Games

The game patterns are listed in the order of their appearance in the book. Each pattern is the size which we have used when making the game.

Make a Soldier

Rag Doll Dress-Up

Feed Benny Bear

Worm Word Circles

A Mug of Synonyms

Catch a Baby Kangaroo

Tasty Homonyms

Find My Grandchildren (Grandfather)

Find My Grandchildren (Grandchild)

Cones for Sale

Rhyming Clowns

Snowmen Match

Help to Brew the Witches' Stews

Hukilau

Early Birds

Catch the Raindrops

Save the Bunnies

Sweet Treats

Trim the Hats

Hoots for Home

Bag Some Peanuts

Knights in Shining Armor

Ghostly Guests

Pancakeman Compounds

A Dog's Life

Lovebirds

Monkey in the Tree

Flying Syllables

Lurking Lions

Prefix Piggies

Suffix Squirrel

Rooty Ant

Willie the Worm

Alphabet Doggies

Play Ball (Player)

Play Ball (Mitt and Ball)

Raggedy Rita's Story Garden (Raggedy Rita)

Raggedy Rita's Story Garden (Heart Flower)

Abbreviation Bunnies

Metric Mice

Play the Centimeter Game

A love of reading paves the way to a love of learning.

MAKE A SOLDIER

RAG DOLL DRESS-UP

FEED BENNY BEAR

HONEYPOT

here

out

in

As soft as...

a pillow

My Pet Rabbit

I have a little
pet. He is soft
and furry. I
play with him
in the back
yard. He has
white fur
and red eyes.

word

•

circle

pet

slit

st

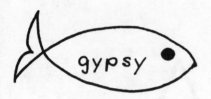

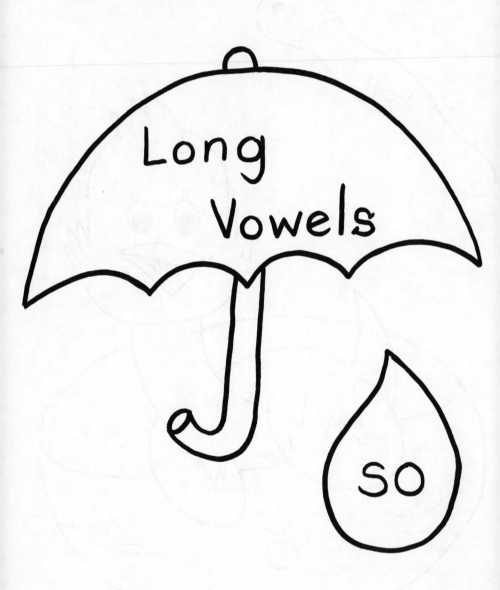

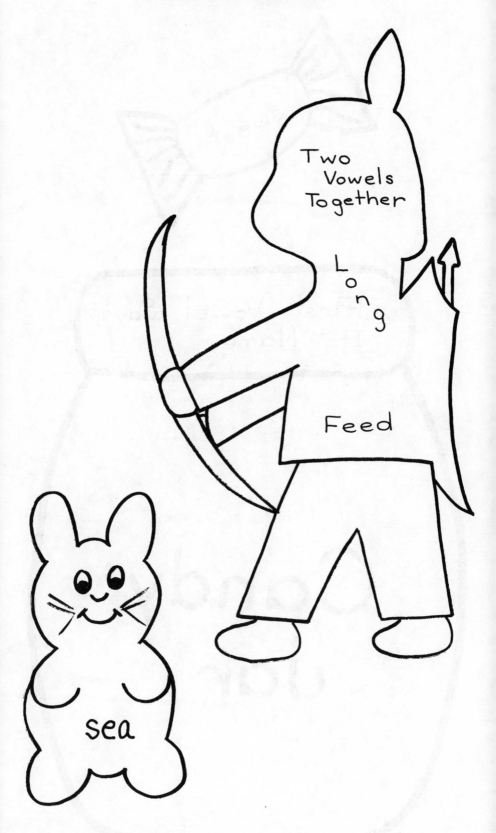

sweet

First Vowel Says
Its Name

Candy
Jar

BAG SOME PEANUTS

sad

sadder
saddest

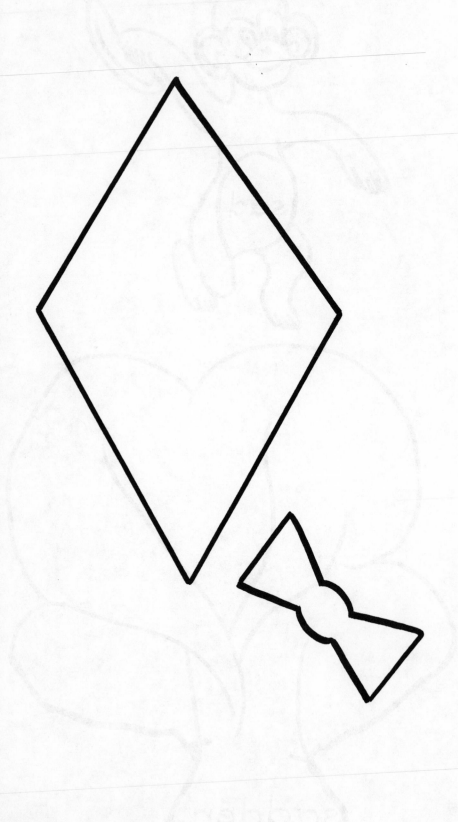

un do

lovely

WILLIE THE WORM

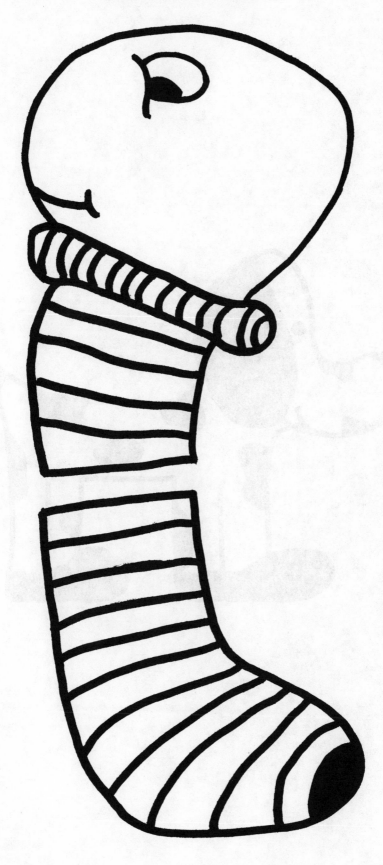

PLAY BALL

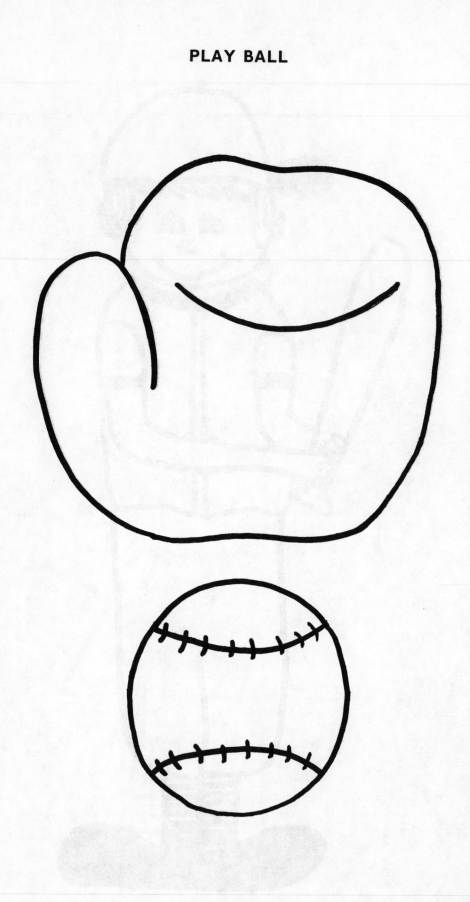

RAGGEDY RITA

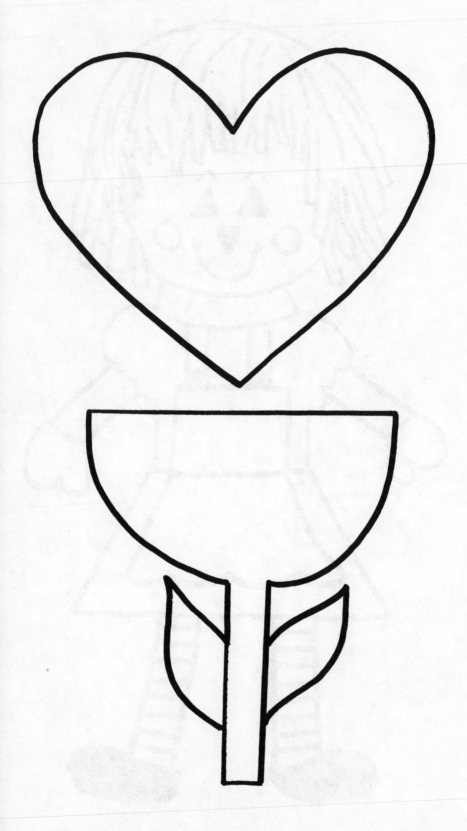

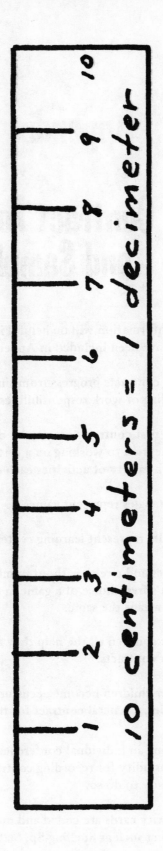

10 centimeters = 1 decimeter

Appendix B:

Contract Forms and Samples

Certain information will be helpful in decoding the contract forms which have been included in Appendix B:

1. The contracts progress from simple coding to more reading of work responsibilities.

2. The first contracts are day by day so that children become used to working on a certain amount of work and a variety of activities each day.

3. Rectangles represent games.

4. Circles represent learning centers.

5. Boxes and circles without numbers represent the student's free choice of a game in that category. A ____ line means the same.

6. Give children all the help they need in carrying out their contracts.

7. After children become accustomed to doing daily activities, a general contract for the week is appropriate.

8. During an individual conference, the teacher takes responsibility for recording contract items until a child is ready to do so.

9. Activity cards are coded and numbered according to subject such as Spelling-Sp, Math-M, and Writing-Wr.

A CONTRACT
This is the work I will do:

<u>September 18 to September 22</u>

1. Monday – Packet, 4 , 17 , Wr 3, 10 .

2. Tuesday – 3 , Packet, 12 , Wr 5, 2 , 🐛 🐛 Filmstrip 2.

3. Wednesday – Packet, 1 , 5 , Draw a picture of an insect. 🦋

4. Thursday – Wr 7, 8 , Packet, 15, 9 .

5. Friday – I.A., 6 , 2 , Packet, 3 , Bake cookies. 🍪🍪

Pupil <u>Jessica</u>

Teacher <u>Miss Burie</u>

A CONTRACT
This is the work I will do:

<u>October 16 - October 20</u>

1. Monday - ■ , Packet, ● 4 , ● ,
■ 18 .

2. Tuesday - ■ 11 , ■ , Packet, ■ 6 .
Happy Birthday, Karl 🎂

3. Wednesday - ■ , ■ 1 , Go to
I.A. To make ⛵.

4. Thursday - Trip to the Farm,
Trip story.

5. Friday - Farm mural work ✏️
■ , ● , Packet , ● 4 .

Pupil ___ Karl

Teacher ___ Miss Burie

I agree to complete this work
for the week of:

October 21 - October 25

1. Monday - Word Cards, Packet, 14,
11.

2. Tuesday - Field trip

3. Wednesday - Friendship Reading, 6,
Work on field trip mural

4. Thursday - Media Center, 12, 23,
3, Packet.

5. Friday - 10, Packet, 8,
Friendship Reading.

Pupil _Jenny_

Teacher _Mrs. Heltshe_

CONTRACT
I agree to complete the following
work for the week of:

November 4 - November 8

1. Monday - ▇ , 11 , 4 , Packet,
   Friendship Reading.

2. Tuesday - Wr 21, 22 , 8 , Go to
   the Art Room to work on
   your stuffed cat.

3. Wednesday - ● , Packet, M— ,12,
   Friendship Reading.

4. Thursday - Wr —, ▇ , Packet, ▇ ,
   Media Center (free choice).

5. Friday - ▇ , Packet, 15 ,
   Friendship Reading.

Pupil _Mary_

Teacher _Mrs. Heltshe_

CONTRACT
I agree to complete this work
for the week of:
__December 14 - December 18__

GAMES

39 , 78 , 82 , 14 , 27 ,

15 , 30 .

ACTIVITY CARDS

Wr 32 , 97 , 36

M 14 , 35 , 79

CENTERS

Rudolph's   Santa's Center

Snowman's Delight 4 , 8 , 6 , 3 .

PACKET

_____ Reading pages each day

_____ Math pages each day

SPELLING CARDS

14 , 10 , 3

SRA

3 cards (gold)

FRIENDSHIP READING

Tuesday , Wednesday , Friday

Pupil ___Amy___

Teacher ___Mrs. Heltshe___

Merry

Christmas!

MY CONTRACT

Name: Roy

Date: February 11 to 15

Games	Stations	Pages to Read
Red: 52, ——, 19		30

		Papers
Blue: ——, 1		5 Reading
		4 Math
		4 Spelling

Games	Projects
Yellow: 3, ——	
Green 48, 17, ——, ——	1. Work on your bird study.
	2. Friday - Sew vest with Mrs. L.
Brown: 3	3. Make a valentine for an elderly friend.

Teacher: Miss Burie

Orange: 20, 26

Be Mine

Happy Valentine's Day!

Pink: ——, ——

190

CONTRACT

I agree to complete this work
for the week of:

March 11 - March 15

Centers	Activity Cards	Packet
15 , 3 , ● , ● . 8 , ● . Piglet's Center 5 , ● .	Wr 19, 32, 14 M 86, 41, 56 Sp 2, 3	_2_ Reading papers each day _2_ Math pages each day

Games	Friendship Reading
Red __15_, _83_, ▨ .	Monday __X__
Blue __33_, _1_, ▨ .	Tuesday _____
Green __3_, ▨ .	Wednesday _X__
Yellow ▨ .	Thursday _____
Orange __11_, ▨ .	Friday __X__
Purple ▨ .	

Special Assignments

1. Go to the I.A. room and work on your doll house.
2. Play Word-o with a friend.
3. Art Room.
4. Finish sewing your skirt.

Pupil __Ann__

Teacher __Mrs. Heltshe__

CONTRACT
I agree to complete this work
for the week of:

April 3 - April 7

Centers	Activity Cards	Packet
⓾, ⑮, 7, ④, Pippi's Center, Pooh's Spelling Center, ㉑, ⑤, ⑭.	Wr 101, 102, 111, ——, ——, M 43, 57, ——, ——. Sp 11, 12, 13.	<u>3</u> Reading pages each day <u>2</u> Math pages each day

Games	Friendship Reading
Red <u>89, 27, 15, 145, 281</u>	Monday _____
Blue <u>23, 29, 100, 18</u>	Tuesday <u>X</u>
Green <u>15, 20</u>	Wednesday _____
Yellow <u>16</u>	
Orange <u>17, 2</u>	Thursday <u>X</u>
Pink <u>38</u>	Friday <u>X</u>

Special Assignments

1. Help bake Easter cake.
2. Art Room: Work on your project.
3. Media Center: Find books and filmstrips about trains.
4. I.A. Room: Finish your hamster cage.

Pupil <u>John</u>

Teacher <u>Mrs. Heltshe</u>

192

Pupil: Leigh
Teacher: Miss Burie
Date: April 6 to April 10

Games	Weekly Musts	Centers
ed 25, ___	___ Read a book.	3 - Let's PreTend
blue 2, 43		
yellow 18, ___	___ Go to the Media Center.	16 - Happy Homonyms
green 35, 23		
range ___	___ 12 papers from your packet.	Choose Two:
brown ___		
pink 45, ___		___
	___ Practice spelling words.	___
Reading		
35 pages		

Activity Cards	Projects
Wr 73, Sp 14, 15 M 36	Wednesday 9:30 A.M. Go to I.A. room to make Kite.

Work with Others or Special Activities

1. I will play a math game with 2 other people.

2. I will do "Buddy Reading" with a friend on Tuesday.

3. I will bake "Shaggy Dogs" on Friday, (2 P.M.).

CONTRACT
I agree to complete this work
for the week of:

April 10 – April 14

Centers	Games	Packet
Charlie Brown's Center 9, 10, 3, 12, ●. Free Choice: ●, ●, ●.	34, 23, 284, 99, 24, 15. Free Choice ■, ■, ■, ■, ■.	_3_ Reading pages each day _2_ Math pages each day

Art Room	Media Center	Activity Cards
Mon. ☐ _____	Mon. ☒ Free Choice	Wr 82, 43, —, —, —.
Tues. ☒ Dinosaur project	Tues. ☐ _____	
Wed. ☐ _____	Wed. ☐ _____	M 18, 21, —, —, —.
Thurs. ☒ Dinosaur project	Thurs. ☐ _____	
Fri. ☐ _____	Fri. ☒ Free Choice	Sp 17, 18, 19.

I. A. Room	Special Assignment
Mon. ☐ _____ Tues. ☐ _____ Wed. ☒ Work on racing car. Thurs. ☐ _____ Fri. ☐ _____	1. Help work on field trip mural. 2. Practice word cards with a friend. 3. Play Spell-It with a group. Pupil ___Phillip___ Teacher ___Mrs. Heltshe___

My Work for:
Monday

1. 92 , 27 .

2. Packet

3. M 33

4. Practice Word Cards.
   no he to

5. Art Room

Pupil __Bobby__

Teacher __Mrs. Heltshe__

This form can be used with
children who are not ready for
a weekly contract.

Skill Index to Games

Many of the games described can be used to reinforce skills other than the skill or skills for which they were originally intended. Therefore, in addition to the basic skills found in the Table of Contents and the more specific skills found in the upper right-hand corner of each new game page, we are including this index which contains a comprehensive, alphabetical listing of reading skills and the games which teach each skill.

ABBREVIATIONS
Abbreviation Bunnies, 122
Birds Fly, 128
Metric Mice, 124

ACCENT MARKS
Clothes Closet, 102

ALPHABET RECOGNITION
Alphabet Puzzle Match, 29
Alphabet Scramble, 29

ALPHABETIZING
Alphabet Doggies, 100
Animal ABC, 40
Spell My Name, 137
Willie the Worm, 99

ANTONYMS
Catch a Baby Kangaroo, 48

AUDITORY
DISCRIMINATION
Matching at the Zoo, 36

BLENDS
Help to Brew the Witches'
Stews, 65

CLASSIFICATION
Dinosaurs at Dinnertime, 133
Food Group Match, 38
Insect Quiz, 129
Match the Screws, 25
Rock Hunt, 132

COLOR WORD RECOGNITION
Color Fun at Pooh Corner, 116
Colorful Pet Shop, 32

COMPARATIVES
Monkey in the Tree, 90

COMPOUND WORDS
Catch That Compound, 84
Compound Fracture, 85
Mend the Broken Hearts, 87
Pancakeperson Compounds, 86

COMPREHENSION
Animal Talk, 112
Cones for Sale, 55
Dinosaurs at Dinnertime, 133

Hornbook, 136
Match the Horses, 107
Metric Measure Up, 127
Nursery Rhyme Jumble, 108
Play Ball, 110
Play the Centimeter Game, 126
The Name Game, 106
Which Worker Am I, 135
Yummy in the Tummy, 104

CONFIGURATION
Take a Ride on Little Toot, 57

CONSONANT BLENDS
Help to Brew the Witches'
Stews, 65
Spell Time, 138

CONSONANT DIGRAPHS
Digraph Fun, 64
Spell Time, 138

CONSONANT SOUNDS
Spell Time, 138
Toyland Jamboree, 62

CONTEXT CLUES
Animal ABC, 40
As Easy as Pie, 54
Cones for Sale, 55
Feed Benny Bear, 41
Find My Grandchildren, 52
Match the Horses, 107
Meanings Galore, 51
Nursery Rhyme Jumble, 108
Watch the Signs, 44
Which Worker Am I, 135
Worm Word Circles, 43
Yummy in the Tummy, 104

CONTRACTIONS
A Dog's Life, 88
Lovebirds, 89

CREATIVE WRITING
Animal Talk, 112
Play Ball, 110
Raggedy Rita's Story Garden,
114

DEFINITIONS
A Mug of Synonyms, 47
Abbreviation Bunnies, 122

Animal Babies, 131
Catch That Compound, 84
Feed Benny Bear, 41
Hornbook, 136
Insect Quiz, 129
Let's Eat, 39
Matching at the Zoo, 36
Metric Mice, 124
Spring Flower Match, 130
The Name Game, 106

DIACRITICAL MARKINGS
Clothes Closet, 102
Diacritical Decisions, 103

DICTIONARY SKILLS
Alphabet Doggies, 100
Animal ABC, 40
Clothes Closet, 102
Diacritical Decisions, 103
Willie the Worm, 99

DIGRAPHS
Digraph Fun, 64

DRAWING CONCLUSIONS
Guess Who Is Here, 118
Hornbook, 136
Rag Doll Dress-Up, 34
Yummy in the Tummy, 104

EYE-HAND MOTOR
COORDINATION
A Breakfast Puzzle, 37
Circle Puzzles, 19
Grid Puzzles, 22
How Many Triangles, 21
Make a Soldier, 20
Rag Doll Dress-Up, 34

FIGURATIVE SPEECH
As Easy as Pie, 54
Find My Grandchildren, 52

FOLLOWING DIRECTIONS
Color Fun at Pooh Corner, 116
Colorful Pet Shop, 32
Metric Measure Up, 127
Rag Doll Dress-Up, 34

GENERALIZATIONS
Animal Talk, 112
Yummy in the Tummy, 104

HOMOGRAPHS
Make a Word Family, 61
Snowpeople Match, 60

HOMONYMS
Tasty Homonyms, 49

INFERENCE
Animal Talk, 112
Cones for Sale, 55
Find the Right Box, 28
Guess Who Is Here, 118
Hornbook, 136
Match the Horses, 107
Play Ball, 110

Raggedy Rita's Story Garden, 114
Which Worker Am I, 135
Yummy in the Tummy, 104

INITIAL CONSONANT
SOUNDS
Toyland Jamboree, 62

INTERPRETING
DESCRIPTIVE WORDS
As Easy as Pie, 54
Find My Grandchildren, 52

LITERATURE
Color Fun at Pooh Corner, 116
Guess Who Is Here, 118

LONG VOWEL SOUNDS
Catch the Raindrops, 71
Diacritical Decisions, 103
Save the Bunnies, 73
Spell Time, 138
Sweet Treats, 75
The Long and Short of It, 69

MAIN IDEAS
Animal Talk, 112
Cones for Sale, 55
Guess Who Is Here, 118
Hornbook, 136
Match the Horses, 107
Raggedy Rita's Story Garden, 114
Yummy in the Tummy, 104

MATHEMATICS
Abbreviation Bunnies, 122
Birds Fly, 128
Buy a Toy, 121
Metric Measure Up, 127
Metric Mice, 124
Play the Centimeter Game, 126
Shopping for Toys, 119

MENTAL DEVELOPMENT
Colorful Pet Shop, 32
Dilemma Dillies, 33
Rag Doll Dress-Up, 34

MULTIPLE MEANINGS
Meanings Galore, 51
Tasty Homonyms, 49

PARAGRAPHS
Cones for Sale, 55
Dinosaurs at Dinnertime, 133
Hornbook, 136
Metric Measure Up, 127

PERCEPTION
Color Fun at Pooh Corner, 116
Colorful Pet Shop, 32
Circle Puzzles, 19
Grid Puzzles, 22
Find the Right Box, 28
How Many Triangles, 21
Make a Soldier, 20
Play the Centimeter Game, 126

Rag Doll Dress-Up, 34
Shape Up, 27

PHONETIC ANALYSIS
Bag Some Peanuts, 79
Catch the Raindrops, 71
Digraph Fun, 64
Early Birds, 67
Help to Brew the Witches'
  Stews, 65
Hoots for Home, 78
Hukilau, 66
Monkey in the Tree, 90
Make a Word Family, 61
Rhyming Clowns, 58
Save the Bunnies, 73
Knights in Shining Armor, 80
Snowpeople Match, 60
Spell My Name, 137
Spell Time, 138
Sweet Treats, 75
The Long and Short of It, 69
Toyland Jamboree, 62
Trim the Hats, 77

PICTURE INTERPRETATION
Animal Babies, 131
Animal Talk, 112
Insect Quiz, 129
Match the Horses, 107
Our Belongings, 83
Play the Centimeter Game, 126
Spring Flower Match, 130
Which Worker Am I, 135

PLURALS
Plural Party, 81

POSSESSIVES
Our Belongings, 83

PREFIXES
Prefix Piggies, 95
Rooty Ants, 97

PROBLEM SOLVING
Dilemma Dillies, 33
Find the Right Box, 28
Metric Measure Up, 127

PRONUNCIATION
Clothes Closet, 102
Diacritical Decisions, 103

READINESS
Alphabet Puzzle Match, 29
Alphabet Scramble, 30
Circle Puzzles, 19
Colorful Pet Shop, 32
Dilemma Dillies, 33
Find the Right Box, 28
Grid Puzzles, 22
How Many Triangles, 21
Make a Soldier, 20
Match the Screws, 25
Rag Doll Dress-Up, 34
Shape Up, 27
Spool Roundup, 24

RHYMING
Make a Word Family, 61
Rhyming Clowns, 58
Snowpeople Match, 60

ROOT WORDS
Monkey in the Tree, 90
Prefix Piggies, 95
Rooty Ants, 97
Suffix Squirrel, 95

SCIENCE
Animal Babies, 131
Dinosaurs at Dinnertime, 133
Insect Quiz, 129
Rock Hunt, 132
Spring Flower Match, 130

SEQUENCE
Nursery Rhyme Jumble, 108

SHORT VOWEL SOUNDS
Catch the Raindrops, 71
Diacritical Decisions, 103
Early Birds, 67
Save the Bunnies, 73
Spell Time, 138
The Long and Short of It, 69

SOCIAL STUDIES
Hornbook, 136
Which Worker Am I, 135

SPELLING
Spell My Name, 137
Spell Time, 138
Yummy in the Tummy, 104

STRUCTURAL ANALYSIS
A Dog's Life, 88
Catch That Compound, 84
Compound Fracture, 85
Count the Syllables, 91
Flying Syllables, 92
Ghostly Guests, 82
Monkey in the Tree, 90
Lovebirds, 89
Lurking Lions, 93
Mend the Broken Hearts, 87
Our Belongings, 83
Pancakeperson Compounds, 86
Plural Party, 81
Prefix Piggies, 95
Rooty Ants, 97
Spell My Name, 137
Spell Time, 138
Suffix Squirrel, 96

SUFFIXES
Rooty Ants, 97
Suffix Squirrel, 96

SYLLABICATION
Count the Syllables, 91
Flying Syllables, 92
Lurking Lions, 93

SYNONYMS
A Mug of Synonyms, 47
Ring the Words, 46

VARIABLE CONSONANT
SOUNDS
Hukilau, 66
Knights in Shining Armor, 80
Spell Time, 138

VARIABLE VOWEL SOUND
Bag Some Peanuts, 79
Hoots for Home, 78
Spell Time, 138

VARIANT INFLECTIONAL
ENDINGS
Ghostly Guests, 82

VISUAL DISCRIMINATION
A Breakfast Puzzle, 37
Alphabet Puzzle Match, 29
Alphabet Scramble, 30
Circle Puzzles, 19
Find the Right Box, 28
Grid Puzzles, 22
Make a Soldier, 20
Match the Screws, 25
Matching at the Zoo, 36
Rag Doll Dress-Up, 34
Shape Up, 27
Spool Roundup, 24

VISUAL MOTOR
Circle Puzzles, 19
How Many Triangles, 21
Make a Soldier, 20

VOWEL DIGRAPHS
Sweet Treats, 75

VOWEL DIPTHONGS
Trim the Hats, 77

VOWEL RULES
Save the Bunnies, 73
Sweet Treats, 75

The Long and Short of It, 69

WORD PERCEPTION
A Breakfast Puzzle, 37
A Mug of Synonyms, 47
Abbreviation Bunnies, 122
Animal ABC, 40
As Easy as Pie, 54
Catch a Baby Kangaroo, 48
Feed Benny Bear, 41
Find My Grandchildren, 52
Food Group Match, 38
Let's Eat, 39
Matching at the Zoo, 36
Meanings Galore, 51
Metric Mice, 124
Ring the Words, 46
Tasty Homonyms, 49
Watch the Signs, 44
Worm Word Circles, 43

WORD RECOGNITION
A Breakfast Puzzle, 37
Abbreviation Bunnies, 122
Animal ABC, 40
Animal Babies, 131
Animal Talk, 112
Birds Fly, 128
Buy a Toy, 121
Catch That Compound, 84
Dinosaurs at Dinnertime, 133
Feed Benny Bear, 41
Food Group Match, 38
Guess Who Is Here, 118
Insect Quiz, 129
Let's Eat, 39
Matching at the Zoo, 36
Metric Mice, 124
Play the Centimeter Game, 126
Rock Hunt, 132
Shopping for Toys, 119
Spring Flower Match, 130
Watch the Signs, 44
Worm Word Circles, 43
Yummy in the Tummy, 104

General Index

The listings in this index concern specific items which pertain to an open approach to learning and to games in particular.

Attracting children to games, 8, 12, 17

Child-centered classroom, 8, 16, 139, 140
Contracting, 10, 11, 17

Decision making, 11, 17, 139-140
Developing work habits, 17, 139-140
Directions, 12, 16

Freedom, 16, 17, 139-140

Independent work skills, 11, 17, 139-140
Individualizing instructions, 10-11, 16, 139

Learning objectives, 10, 139

Origin of games, 8, 139-140

Parent involvement, 12, 139, 140
Peer teaching, 11, 12, 140
Protecting games, 13, 17

Responsibility, 16, 17, 139-140
Room arrangement, 10, 16, 17

Scheme for coding, 11, 12, 16-17
Skill sequence, 10-11, 139-140
Storage ideas, 12, 17

Teacher-aide involvement, 12, 139
Time saving, 12, 13, 14

Photo Courtesy—National Education Association Publishing Joe Di Dio